CHAMPIONS OF THE INDIANAPOLIS 500

The Men Who Have Won More Than Once

CHAMPIONS OF THE INDIANAPOLIS 500

The Men Who Have Won More Than Once

By BILL LIBBY

ILLUSTRATED WITH PHOTOGRAPHS

DODD, MEAD & COMPANY

NEW YORK

The photographs in this book are courtesy of:

Bob Tronolone: pages 94, 95, 96 top, 97 bottom, 98, 99 top, 100 top, 101 bottom, 102 bottom, 103; *Ted Wilson:* pages 33 top, 34; *John W. Posey:* pages 40 top, 101 top; *J. M. Stitt:* page 95 top; *George Rose:* page 99 bottom; *USAC:* page 100 bottom; *Bud Jones:* page 102 top. All others courtesy of Indianapolis Motor Speedway.

Library of Congress Cataloging in Publication Data

Libby, Bill.
  Champions of the Indianapolis 500.

  Includes index.
  1. Automobile racing—United States—Biography.
2. Indianapolis Speedway Race. I. Title.
GV1032.A1L5   796.7'2'0922 [B]   76-87
ISBN 0-396-07306-9

For Bob and Susan Storwick
Friends when a fellow needs a friend

A C K N O W L E D G M E N T S

The author wishes to thank Al Bloemker and Charlene Ellis of the Indianapolis Motor Speedway, Jim Cook and Sue Ovitt of the Ontario Motor Speedway, Brian Tracy, Bob Thomas, Hank Ives, Bob Shafer and the other racing writers and publicists who have helped me know the drivers, the drivers who have been kind enough to give me interviews over the years, and Bob Tronolone, John Posey and the photographers whose work appears within these pages. Without these and others like them, a writer could not come close enough to the races and the racers to write about them.

Contents

CHAMPIONS OF THE INDIANAPOLIS 500

The Men Who Have Won More Than Once

1   *Tommy Milton*

1921, 1923 *

The first driver to win the Indianapolis 500 more than once was Tommy Milton, a handsome, modest daredevil of "The Roaring Twenties" who succeeded where such skilled competitors as Ralph DePalma and Dario Resta could not in his time, and as only Louis Meyer, Wilbur Shaw, Mauri Rose, Bill Vukovich, Rodger Ward, A. J. Foyt and Al and Bobby Unser could in later times.

The race drivers of the earlier era were in a way more wonderful than those that followed. Most people did not even know how to drive. The average automobile was slow, awkward and fragile. The early race cars had delicate engines, erratic steering, primitive braking, weak wheels and skimpy tires. The first racetracks consisted of rutty dirt, bumpy bricks or splintering boards.

Imaginative engineers, fascinated by cars, speed and racing, swiftly and steadily improved these machines, and daring drivers pushed them to their limits. Few are aware how fast these first cars could be driven. Shortly before 1900 the listed mile record was less than 40 miles per hour. But, by 1904, Henry Ford had driven a car over a frozen lake at 90 miles per hour. Two years later, the record was lifted to 125 miles per hour. By 1910, Barney Oldfield

* Shared the victory with Howdy Wilcox.

1

had set the speed standard for the measured mile at more than 130 miles per hour, and a year later, Red Burman pushed it past the 140 mph mark.

These speed records were set in straight runs, but men negotiated the original oval racetracks at around 100 miles per hour in the first ten years of the twentieth century. Even at lesser speeds the early cars easily went out of balance, rolled over, caught fire, exploded or broke up in bits as they careened over rough courses. And the drivers, who were not strapped into their cars and did not wear fire-retardant uniforms and crash helmets, were seriously injured or killed as easily as they are today at more than twice the speed.

The names of the men who developed the early engines and cars remain magic—Ford, Chevrolet, Olds, Duesenberg, Firestone, Stutz, Miller, Goosen, Offenhauser and Champion. Some laid the foundation for financial empires in the automotive field. But it is the names of the first daring race drivers that truly capture the imagination—Harroun, Resta, DePalma, DePaolo, Cooper, Murphy and Milton. As all racing drivers are, these were men unlike other men. These are athletes who risk their lives in their sport.

The first "horseless carriages" came into existence in Germany in 1885, and men have raced motorcars ever since. Less than ten years later the Marquis de Dion, in a steam-powered creation, won what was probably the first real car race, a 78-mile road race in France. The development of the internal combustion engine by Duryea, Ford, Olds and others in the United States in the 1890's accelerated racing. The first real race in the United States was William Vanderbilt's 302-mile Vanderbilt Cup Classic through Long Island in 1904. It was won in 6 hours and 45 minutes by Henry Heath.

Many of the major races of the early era were contested at 200 or more miles and were as much a test of the durability of the drivers as of their machines. Even if they kept their cars erect and free of crashes, they usually were pelted by dirt, rocks, splinters and other debris as they went, and their races went on for hours. The first 500 at Indianapolis lasted almost seven hours, much more than twice the time it takes today.

Many major racetracks have been built since, especially in the past twenty years. On these, major races of 400 to 600 miles are run, many of them mainly for stock cars, which are improved versions of the cars we drive on the streets and highways. However, the Indianapolis track, now more than 65 years of age, and its 500-mile race for pure racers, remains set apart from all others in glamour, history and tradition.

More modern tracks have sprung up for Indianapolis cars in Ontario, California, and Pocono, Pennsylvania. High-speed ovals for stock cars have spread throughout the South. The Daytona 500 in Florida is rising rapidly in national appeal. Since World War II, road courses on which sports car classics are conducted have attracted popular events. In recent years, there has been an explosion of interest in the dragsters that sprint down short stretches. Since early in the century, glamorous Grand Prix races, conducted primarily in Europe, have earned enormous interest.

Still, no single sporting event in the world attracts the paid attendance or pays off the sort of purses as Indianapolis. More than a million persons pay to see the practices, trial runs and race annually in May. Around 300,000 persons pay to see the race itself near month's end. About a million dollars is paid out in prizes. Approximately $250,000 goes to the winner. So, men are ready to risk more in this one than in any other. Most American drivers would rather win this one than any other. It is set apart from all the others.

The Indianapolis Motor Speedway was put together as a test track by a group headed by Carl Fisher, a former bicycle-racing champion, who had made his money selling bikes. Later he made much more money with the development of the first automobile headlight and then the development of Miami Beach as a luxury resort area. He made little money from the Indianapolis track, although it was a success with the speed-hungry public from the first. It cost $250,000 to lay out the 2½-mile rectangular closed oval course. It has remained a model for other tracks. Except for changes in the surface of the track and in the surrounding stands, it has remained the same slightly banked oval, keeping constant for purposes of comparison the improvements in cars and speeds.

Originally the track was a dirt course. Barney Oldfield set the first track record there at 76 miles per hour. Bob Burman won the first feature race there at an average speed of 53 miles per hour for 250 miles. But a driver and a mechanic were killed in that inaugural event before a crowd of 60,000 spectators. There were five deaths in the first three days of racing. The public was shocked. Swiftly, the rutty dirt was covered over by bricks as a safety measure.

The first Indianapolis 500 in 1911 drew a crowd of 80,000 fans and paid a purse of $27,550. The first 500 was contested at close to 90 miles per hour, but the fastest cars burned out or broke down. Conserving his car at an average speed of less than 75 miles per hour, a former ribbon clerk, Ray Harroun, receiving relief help from Cyril Patschke in the middle stages of the marathon, outlasted the others and brought his black and gold Marmon Wasp home in front. He retired in Victory Lane. His check came to $14,000.

Most drivers raced with mechanics seated by their side, ready to make repairs on the spot, but the rebel Ray Harroun had a car with a single-seat cockpit. It also had a rear-view mirror, thus starting the track's reputation as a proving ground for passenger car equipment. The Marmon car became so popular that it was withdrawn from future races rather than risk its reputation.

In the following year, 1912, qualifying speeds neared 90 miles per hour. Joe Dawson won that second Indianapolis 500 in a National.

Jules Goux of France won in 1913 in a Peugeot to start a cycle of 500's that were dominated by foreign drivers, including another

Frenchman, Rene Thomas, who won in 1914 in a Delage, and the Italian Dario Resta, who won in 1916 in another Peugeot. Most of the early winners required relief help, but Resta required only chilled champagne, delivered to the pits by his countrymen in the stands, and drunk during stops to replace tires and fill up with fuel.

"Without the good wine, I would not have been able to win," the Frenchman remarked in Victory Lane.

Italian-born Ralph DePalma won the 500 in 1915, but he is considered the first great American race driver. Although he was born in Troia, Italy, in 1883, he moved with his family to New York City when he was ten, was reared in this country and raced here. He won twenty-six championship trail races in his career, the most anyone would win until the 1960's, and two national driving titles, in 1912 and 1914. He also won many other major races.

A handsome sportsman, a hero to the sporting public of his era, DePalma would have made a marvelous subject for this book, but he won at Indianapolis only once. It is those who conquered this classic test of man and machine more than once who have been singled out for preference in these pages.

Indy has been a deadly enemy to drivers. In its first sixty years, thirty-six drivers were killed here, including two who had won the race. Many more were injured seriously. Many immortal racers were frustrated by failures to win here. The first three-time national driving champion, Earl Cooper, drove here seven times without winning. Another three-time national champion, Ted Horn, tried ten times and was second, third or fourth the last nine times without winning.

Two-time national titlist Rex Mays drove here a dozen times without winning, although he captured the pole position as the fastest first-day qualifier a record four times and led a record nine races. Two-time national titlist Tony Bettenhausen tried and failed in fourteen 500's. Cliff Bergere drove more 500's, sixteen, than any man until the 1970's, and more miles—more than 6,100—in this race than any man until A. J. Foyt, but he never finished first.

Indeed, many superstars of this sport have come close countless times, but had to be satisfied with winning only once, including three-time national champions Jimmy Bryan and Mario Andretti, two-time national titlist Jimmy Murphy, and two-time pole-sitter Parnelli Jones.

DePalma himself, the 1915 winner, was called "The King of the Roaring Road," but he called himself "The Hard-Luck King" because he led almost every Indianapolis 500 he entered, but broke down in most of them. He placed on the Indianapolis pole twice, and he led at Indianapolis a record total of 613 laps. But he won only once.

In 1912, DePalma led by five laps with five laps left, but a rod broke in his engine and tore a hole in his crankshaft. Losing oil, he limped toward the finish line as Joe Dawson drove his car past him again and again. When his car came to a stop, less than a mile from the finish, DePalma and his mechanic got out and pushed, but Dawson kept driving around and around until he caught up and came home first.

The picture of DePalma pushing his car through the stretch remains one of the standouts of sports. He was one of those men who became a greater hero in defeat than in victory. Before he finally won in 1915, another rod snapped not far from the finish and he barely limped under the checkered flag before rivals could catch him.

In 1919, DePalma led at the halfway point, but a wheel collapsed under him. A year later he got off far behind when he flatted a tire at the start, but he caught up and led by five miles with thirty miles to go before his engine exploded in flames. His nephew and riding mechanic, Peter DePaolo, crawled onto the hood and put out the flames with a fire extinguisher. Then the car ran out of fuel. Two years later, DePalma led at the halfway mark again when his engine blew up. If he often was an unlucky loser, he was lucky enough to win once, however.

The race was not run in 1917 and 1918 because of World War I.

Howdy Wilcox ended the string of foreign-born winners in 1919 as qualifying speeds soared past 100 miles per hour. Gaston Chevrolet frustrated runnerup Rene Thomas's bid for a second Indianapolis success the following year. In 1921, Tommy Milton made his way to the top. A year later he broke down early as his archrival, Jimmy Murphy, captured the classic. But in 1923, Milton returned to become the first two-time winner of this wonderfully frustrating carnival of speed.

Milton was born in Mt. Clemens, Michigan, in 1893, and he grew up with the horseless carriage. First, he wanted to own one. Then he wanted to race one. He went to work in Minnesota, saved his money and got his own Mercer. Then he went racing with it with Alex Sloan's barnstorming thrill circus, which toured the country running rigged races.

Milton once recalled, "It was 1913. I was just a kid who wanted to race and I happened to have my own Mercer. Sloan brought his show to St. Paul. He offered me a job with his fakeroo outfit. He would pay me fifty dollars a week. As soon as we left and hit the open road, he cut my salary to thirty-five dollars a week. That was his style. There was one eight-day period when we traveled three thousand miles and raced in five cities. For thirty-five dollars a week. No prize money."

Tommy wouldn't have won any money, anyway. He wasn't supposed to win. No one worked on his car to make it a winner. Louis Disbrow was the star of the show. His car was souped-up and he usually won. If another car was working better on a given day, it was supposed to drop back and let Louis win, anyway.

"I stuck it out for three years," Milton recalled. His patience ran out in St. Paul when his sister and her husband came out to see the kid race and he ran so far behind he was booed. "Those bums in the stands got to me," Milton said. He went to work on his car. The tour went to its last stop of the season, in Shreveport, Louisiana, where he won. And was fired.

"It was well worth it," he grinned, years later.

Even losing rigged races, he gained experience in racing and skills in a racing car. Those barnstorming troupes turned out some of the best of the early drivers, including not only Disbrow, but "Terrible Teddy" Tetzlaff, Red Burman and Barney Oldfield. All of them tried Indianapolis but failed to win there.

A year after he was fired from the thrill circus, Milton hooked up with the Duesenberg racing team and landed the sort of rides even the best of drivers needs to win.

Fred and Augie Duesenberg came to this country from Germany as young men in the late 1890's. Fred became a record-setting racer of bicycles in the Midwest. When cars came along, they captured his fancy. He mastered the mechanics of them while working for others, then went into business for himself, with his brother. They used racing to promote their new car. Milton swiftly became the star of their team, which also included Eddie O'Donnell, Eddie Hearne and Eddie Rickenbacker, who became a flying hero.

Before long, he met the man who was to become his most serious competitor. Jimmy Murphy, a former motorcycle racer from Los Angeles. Murphy had been hanging around garages frequented by drivers in an effort to hook up with a car-racing team. Eddie O'Donnell brought him onto the Duesenberg crew to ride as his mechanic. Ambitious and aggressive, Murphy latched onto the star of the team, Milton, and soon was driving with him.

Theirs was an uncommon coupling. Milton was a handsome, polished fellow, modest and shy, while Murphy was homely and crude, cocky but a charmer. But Milton befriended Murphy and taught him a lot about driving and about life. Milton talked Fred Duesenberg into giving Murphy a chance as a driver, but Murphy crashed two cars and was demoted to mechanic again.

Murphy sat alongside Milton as he made his first 500 start at Indianapolis in 1919, but a rod broke in the engine of their "Dusie" at 150 miles and the car placed twenty-fifth while Howdy Wilcox went on to win.

Driving with another mechanic in a race at Uniontown, New Jersey, early the next year, Milton was far ahead of runnerup Gaston Chevrolet when the "Dusie" caught fire speeding down the mainstretch. Milton slammed on the brakes, which bent. The car swayed and rolled over. One of Milton's legs was pinned in the wreckage.

Milton was rushed to the hospital, where doctors wanted to amputate the crushed leg. Milton refused them permission. "I did not want to live with one leg because I did not see how I could drive with one leg. Racing was my life," he later remarked. He was right, too, because the limb mended, though he did spend two months in the hospital.

Murphy visited him there. Discouraged, Murphy talked of giving up racing and returning home. Feeling for the young man, Milton promised to talk to the Duesenbergs about giving Murphy another chance as a driver. Milton said he would threaten to quit the team if Murphy wasn't given another chance. Thus threatened, the Duesenbergs agreed. Murphy began to drive again. And he began to win.

Milton had invested much of his own money in a car the Duesenbergs were preparing for an assault on DePalma's land-speed record over the sand in Daytona Beach, Florida. Almost recovered from his injuries, Milton sent Murphy on to Daytona to help prepare and test the car. The car was ready before Milton was. At the urging of Fred Duesenberg, Murphy took the car out for a trial run and ran faster than 151 miles per hour, surpassing DePalma's record speed of 149.

Milton was on his way south when he read headlines hailing Murphy's feat. He was infuriated. He felt he had befriended the young man and gotten him his chance. He had spent his savings on the project and was paying Murphy's salary to assist him in it. Yet the young man had risked Milton's investment and grabbed glory from him. "I don't think the world ever had looked so black. I could have killed him," Milton said of Murphy later. At Daytona the two argued and went their separate ways to become bitter rivals.

Immediately, Milton took the car out for a run at the record, but fell short. A newspaper reporter wrote that Murphy was Milton's superior and if Duesenberg wanted the record, the car would have to be driven by Murphy, which further infuriated Milton. He camped out in a tent, which protected the car from the damp salt air and sand, while he worked on the racer. He then took it out, put it to its limits, and blasted across the beach at a satisfying new record speed of better than 156 miles per hour.

In a hungry search to better his record, Milton continued on, but his engine exploded and caught fire. Calmly, Milton drove it into the ocean to douse the flames. He was a marvelous driver— daring and durable, calm and canny.

This was the start of the 1920's—"The Golden Age of American Sports." This country had turned from the horrors of World War I to a time of peace and pleasure, and its idols, like Lindbergh, were to loom larger than life. Athletic heroes such as baseball's Babe Ruth, football's Red Grange, boxing's Jack Dempsey, golf's Bobby Jones and tennis's Bill Tilden would be celebrated beyond reason. Car racing sought a superstar, too. It might have been Milton. Instead it became the duel for dominance between Milton and Murphy.

The two teammates took turns in the speed spotlight, former friends who refused to speak to one another off the track and dueled with one another daringly on the track. The Indianapolis 500 became the main battleground for their racing war. Milton won the race in 1921. Murphy won it in 1922. Milton won it again in 1923. Murphy had captured the pole position in 1922. Milton took it in 1923. Murphy took it back in 1924. Milton won the national title in 1920 and 1921. He was the first driver to win it two times in a row. Murphy went out and won it in 1922 and 1924.

DePalma remained the dominant driver as the 1920's opened, but his time at the top was running out. He was favored in the 500

in 1920 and was far in front with only 35 miles left when his engine went sour and he slowed. Gaston Chevrolet's Monroe and
Rene Thomas's Ballot sped past to finish first and second. The
durable "Dusies" of Milton and Murphy followed in third and
fourth places, lacking the speed to contend for the front. DePalma
limped in fifth. The winner's car was the first to run the route without a change of tires, starting a long run of forty years at the top
for Firestone.

Disturbed by his Duesenberg's lack of speed and the cold war
with teammate Murphy, Milton left the team. He wanted his own
car. He borrowed a chassis from Cliff Durant and $5,000 from
Barney Oldfield so the imaginative Harry Miller could make him
an engine. The task was not completed in time for the 1921 Indianapolis renewal. The driving death of Gaston Chevrolet in a California race opened up a seat in the Chevrolet brothers' Frontenac
car and Tommy slid into it. It looked like a fat cigar on wheels.

Again, DePalma's Ballot was too fast for Milton's car, but the
pace was too fast for DePalma's car and those of other contenders.
Murphy's hands were badly burned when his "Dusie" caught fire.
Contender after contender was sidelined. Milton, who had been up
all night rebuilding his engine, found he could remain running
only if he kept below the 100-mile-per-hour mark. But he fell two
laps behind before the engine in DePalma's car burned out shortly
after the midway mark in the marathon.

At this point, Milton in his Chevrolet Frontenac and Roscoe
Sarles in one of the Duesenberg team entries, who had been dueling for second, found themselves dueling for first. Milton led, but
Sarles was saving his car for a final run at the flag. Milton realized
Sarles's car was stronger and speedier. But he knew Sarles was
scarred from accidents. As they neared the finish, Milton decided
to resort to psychological tactics. "I figured I could risk tricking
him. I knew him and I knew what might work with him," he explained later.

In the closing laps, as Sarles closed in on him, Milton slowed slightly to allow the other driver to catch him. As Sarles swept even, Milton turned to look at the other driver, seemed surprised to see him, smiled confidently, patted the tail end of his car, and risked his engine by accelerating away hard. Discouraged, Sarles dropped back and did not again challenge the leader. Later, he insisted to a furious Fred Duesenberg that he was bushed, while Milton was fresh, so why risk a safe second-place payoff in a futile fight for first?

Milton laughed when told this. "You drive with your head as well as the seat of your pants," he said as he accepted the winner's check for $36,000. He, Louis Chevrolet and their team spent the night celebrating their first 500 triumph.

Meanwhile, Murphy mourned the fates. He had talked the Duesenbergs into entering him and a team in the prestigious French Grand Prix. In practice for the race, the brakes on his car locked as he applied them at a turn. The car skidded and overturned, trapping Murphy underneath and cracking his ribs. He was hospitalized.

His burned hands still sore from his Indianapolis mishap of a month earlier, his cracked ribs still sore from his accident of a few days earlier, Murphy was taken from the hospital just two hours before the start of the Grand Prix and lifted from a wheelchair into the cockpit of his car.

Murphy drove daringly around the rugged ten-mile road course and into the lead as it took time for DePalma's engine to take hold. In the last stages, DePalma was closing in, but Murphy hung on to win in a car crippled by a flat tire and a fractured radiator. It was the first foreign victory for an American driver and there would not be another comparable one for forty years.

With this triumph Murphy became the hero of the American racing public, although Milton became the more accomplished driver. Murphy rubbed in his triumph by putting one of the new Miller engines in a Duesenberg and renaming it "The Murphy Special." With it he easily won the pole position at Indianapolis in 1922 and the race as well, while Milton's new Miller Durant expired at 110 miles. This victory helped Murphy end Milton's two-year reign as national driving champion. On top of this, Murphy moved into a Durant.

Pestered by Murphy's public popularity, frustrated by his own failures, Milton worked long and hard with Miller to put together their own streamlined car for 1923, the first in years that did not require a riding mechanic. Milton drove without one in a bitter battle with his old riding mechanic, Murphy. First he surpassed Murphy's old speed record in the time trials, taking the pole position at more than 108 miles per hour. Then he wore Murphy down in a duel for the lead, which changed hands ten times in the first 100 miles.

Milton maneuvered in, through and out of the turns more skillfully, until Murphy's tires began to wear severely and he started to drop back. Then Milton had difficulties of another sort. A dandy, he had attired himself in a brand-new all-white driving outfit. He had replaced his old shoes. He had replaced his comfortable old gloves with a new pair of white kidskin gloves. He had even replaced the black friction tape on his steering wheel with white adhesive tape. As the race wore on, his new shoes began to pinch his feet, his new gloves began to blister his hands, and the tape on his steering wheel began to slip. He tore off his gloves and drove on in agony.

Far ahead at the midway mark, Milton was not sure how long he could go on. When he pitted, he showed his hands to Howdy Wilcox, who offered to take over for a few laps. Milton agreed and hopped out while Howdy hopped in. Milton ran off to get his old shoes and to get his blistered hands taped, while Wilcox drove off. While Milton was gone, Wilcox could not hold the lead. Milton returned in time to see his car being passed by Harry Hartz. Wilcox was called in and the car was refueled. Milton returned to the cockpit after 49 laps on the sidelines, with 49 laps left.

He charged onto the track, caught and passed Hartz and began to pull away. Murphy moved up to challenge Hartz for second place. Milton pulled away from them. At the finish Milton was far in front, with Hartz and Murphy second and third, respectively. The Milton team earned $28,500 of the $83,000 purse, as well as a place in posterity.

Ten years had elapsed before the infant classic had its first two-time winner and another ten would elapse before it had another. Grease-smeared, sore and weary, the marvel Milton exulted in Victory Lane, "That's one for the record books! Now for number three!"

Number three never came.

Bent on revenge, Murphy followed Milton into master-builder Miller's cars in 1924. He beat out Hartz and Milton for the pole position in that year's 500. However, the Duesenbergs had developed for their cars a new engine with the first supercharger ever used at the Speedway, and Studebaker had turned out a tremendous racer. At the outset of the race, the great Earl Cooper in a Studebaker pulled away from all but Murphy in his Miller and steadily widened his margin on Murphy. Meanwhile, Milton's car came apart and the best of the Duesenberg drivers, Joe Boyer, had his beast break down on him.

At the 300-mile mark, Fred Duesenberg returned Boyer to the race, replacing driver Slim Corum in another Dusie. The car was better than it had been driven, and Boyer began to pick off the cars in front of him. He closed ground on the leaders, lap after lap. As he applied pressure to the leaders, they pressed their cars to their limits. At 350 miles, Boyer was within 33 seconds of Murphy, who skidded out of contention, tearing up a tire. At 400 miles, he was within 44 seconds of Cooper, who risked running hard on bad rubber. At 450 miles, Boyer burst into the lead as Cooper pitted with a torn tire.

Cooper came back to battle Boyer through the last laps in a spectacular race that had the fans standing and screaming for their favorites. With 30 miles left, Cooper caught Boyer. But as he began to go by Boyer in the first turn, Cooper lost control of his car and skidded dangerously, tearing up another tire before he could regain control. He had to pit for new rubber. By then, Boyer was out of reach. Boyer came in first, with Cooper second and Murphy third. Milton had long since retired to the sidelines.

Murphy's Miller was superior to Milton's. As they drove along the championship trail that year, Murphy won more often than Milton, piling up the points he needed to capture a second national title to match Milton's. Murphy won at Kansas City and Altoona; Milton won at Charlotte. The tour took them to the one-mile dirt track at Syracuse in upstate New York. Murphy did not like to drive on dirt and seldom did, but in his hunger to pile up points to protect his lead in the driving standings, he did so this day, the fifteenth of September, 1924.

Milton did not mind driving on dirt. He was not bothered by the things that bothered Murphy. Milton had few superstitions, Murphy many. One superstition Murphy had was that he not make travel arrangements until after each race, as if it would jinx him to assume he would get through the race safely. But this afternoon, his sponsor had a commitment that compelled him to leave early, so he had purchased Murphy's train ticket before the race. He pressed it on the protesting Murphy. As if he felt a fool for making too much of it, Murphy shrugged and tucked the tickets into his pocket.

In the race, he crashed into a fence, and a splinter of wood drove into his heart, killing him at the age of thirty.

Milton was moved deeply by the death of his former friend and long-time foe. Apparently he regretted the grudge he had carried against the other driver all those years, although he refused to talk about it. Years later, he did sigh and say, "It was a waste."

At the track that day, the race no longer mattered to him. He wept privately. Then he asked for and received permission to accompany the body back to California. There, he made the funeral arrangements for Murphy and paid most of the expenses for the burial of his fallen rival. Tears streamed down Milton's face as Murphy was lowered into the ground.

Drivers die, but the races go on. Phil Shafer had won that race at Syracuse; others won other races through the season. Cooper won enough points to almost capture his fourth national title, but he fell short in the end. Murphy's total held up and he was awarded posthumously the prize he had wanted so much.

Milton went on for a while, but he won only one more major race, on the boards at Culver City, California. He drove in two more 500's, but did not challenge for the lead. Never again was he in contention for the national title. Something had gone out of him which he could not get back. He loved driving and hated the thought of retirement, but once he stopped winning there seemed no point in running the risks.

Peter DePaolo won Indy in 1925, the fabulous Frank Lockhart in 1926, George Souders in 1927. Tommy Milton drove his eighth and last race at Indianapolis in 1927. But he could not stay away from the race. He returned to serve as an official at the track and was chief steward for many years before his death in 1962.

Milton was typical of many drivers who are hooked on this mean narcotic of car racing and cannot shake it no matter how many painful experiences they have endured. He once said, "The hardest job I've ever had is being a retired race driver. I want to drive every race I see. And I see every race I can. I can't stay away from the track, even though it's torture to be there."

The first two-time champion of the Indianapolis 500, a key figure in the most famous feud in American car-racing history, Tommy Milton retired in the 1920's, concluding a quarter-century of pioneering in which the first great race drivers arrived. It marked the end of one golden era in this spectacular sport and the beginning of another in which another duel of great drivers developed, though not as bitter and tragic a one as the other had been.

2 *Louis Meyer*

1928, 1933, 1936

The first three-time winner of the Indianapolis 500 was Louis Meyer. He drove a dozen years at Indy and captured the classic contest in 1928, 1933 and 1936. He finished second in 1929, and fourth in 1930 and 1937. He continued to compete until 1939, when he broke through the "barrier" of 130 miles per hour at "the Brickyards" in the qualifying time-trials, but wrecked in the race. He retired after struggling from his smashed racer.

Meyer was a marvelous race-car driver, but he was not a "charger," so he was not colorful. He planned his races and displayed patience. Often he waited for the cars of the more reckless drivers to break before he made his move. He seldom paced Indy in qualifying, but he usually was not far from the pace on race day. He was consistent along the championship trail and won the national driving title in consecutive seasons in 1928 and 1929 and again in 1933.

Louie Meyer was born in July, 1904, in lower Manhattan. His father had been a bicycle racer in France who had come to this country in 1895 and become a barber. After a fling in Florida, the elder Meyer settled his family in California, going first into the restaurant business, then into real estate in Los Angeles. Louie had an older brother, Eddie, who loved cars and speed and hooked his younger brother on racing.

After Eddie took a Ford to triumph in a road race in Ontario, outside of Los Angeles, where an Indianapolis-style track later was built, Louie began to travel the racing tour with his brother. Louie kept asking for a chance to drive, and Eddie kept saying he couldn't handle a car at speed. Finally, Louie got on a track with Eddie's car and drove it faster than Eddie had.

Before long, Louie was racing on the tour that had sprung up in those days, and Eddie had dropped out. Louie had a spectacular career, which crossed Wilbur Shaw's. Their spectacular rivalry matched that of Tommy Milton and Jimmy Murphy, though without the bitterness.

Meyer and Shaw dominated the American racing scene in the late 1920's and especially through most of the 1930's in a way that never has been surpassed. However, because Shaw was more of a charger, more colorful, he became the bigger popular hero, although it was not until Meyer's career was waning that Shaw attained the top position.

Many ironies were involved with their debuts at Indianapolis. They arrived there the same year, 1927. Shaw had a ride, Meyer did not. Shaw's sponsor had purchased the car that had carried Jimmy Murphy to his death. Meyer had helped rebuild it and was hired to serve as a mechanic on it. It was a slow but strong car, which vibrated badly on the rough brick road. Shaw was shaken so severely that he accepted relief help from Meyer for more than 125 miles in midrace. Shaw returned to finish fourth as most of the front-runners folded and an outsider, George Souders, sneaked in with his Duesenberg.

The following year, Meyer's first start at Indy came in a car he grabbed right out from under Shaw. Wilbur's backer had entered him in a new Miller Special, but when expected sponsorship support fell through, he decided to sell the car. Shaw sought a new backer to buy it, but Meyer beat him to it with Alden Sampson backing him. Sadly, Shaw settled for a last-minute ride in a car wrecked by Peter DePaolo in the time trials. It was rebuilt and allowed to qualify far back in the field on the morning of race day. The engine failed after 100 miles, however, and that was that. Meanwhile, Meyer and his Miller performed marvelously.

Frank Lockhart had died at Daytona earlier in the year. All Lockhart's Speedway standards then were surpassed in the mid-May time trials at Indy. In the race itself, Leon Duray, who had led the qualifiers with a one-lap speed of close to 130 miles per hour and a four-lap average above 120, sped far in front over the first 160 miles before his overworked engine overheated and he started to drop back. Tony Gulotta, Jimmy Gleason, George Souders and Babe Stapp then traded the lead back and forth for another 260 miles before a brief bit of drizzling rain slowed and bunched the field under the caution flag for a few laps.

The fast pace had punished the leaders' machines. Lou Meyer and Lou Moore, both in Millers, had been biding their time to conserve their cars. After the cars were sent away at speed again, they began to move up with less than a fifth of the marathon remaining. In turn they passed Stapp, then Souders as a wave of anticipation swept across the crowd. With 45 miles left, Gleason led Gulotta, Meyer and Moore in that order. Gulotta's engine started to starve for fuel from a clogged line. As he slowed, first Meyer, then Moore swept past him.Gleason's engine was misfiring from electrical problems, but he hung on until only five laps were left. At that point, he hurried into the pits for help. His desperate crew poured water on his magneto, which finished him.

Suddenly, then, Meyer led, with Moore pressing him. They thundered through the last laps as the excitement mounted. Meyer refused to give ground. He hung on to his advantage and flashed across the finish line well in front after more than five hours of fury.

At the age of twenty-three, virtually a rookie, in his first start at the fabled "Brickyards," Meyer was a winner. Pushing his aviator goggles high on his grease-smeared face in Victory Lane, he wearily allowed that it was a "wonderful feeling."

An unemotional man, he seemed to take his stunning upset triumph in stride. "I hope it will be the first of many," he said matter-of-factly as he accepted the first-place prize of $28,500 from a $90,000 purse provided by former racer and war hero Eddie Rickenbacker, who had presided over his first race. Rickenbacker headed the group that had purchased the Speedway from Carl Fisher for less than $1 million. The Indianapolis 500 had entered a new era and Lou Meyer was to be the first dominant figure.

Meyer won also at Altoona that year and the next in 200-mile races, came close to capturing the 500 a second successive time the next year, and piled up sufficient points to win the national driving championship both years.

In the 1929 Indianapolis renewal, Meyer and his Miller stuck close to the lead for half the race, moved in front at the midway mark, and were way ahead when the engine stalled on the last pit stop. Meyer sat in frustration in the cockpit of the car for seven minutes, which seemed an eternity, while his crew worked frantically to restart the car. By the time they got it going, the cars of Ray Keech and Lou Moore had moved into the lead. Keech captured the classic when Moore's engine gave way with only five miles left. Meyer had been so far in front of the rest that despite his long delay he still came in second.

His "running time" on the track had been by far the fastest in the field, but he accepted defeat gracefully. "You can't run if your engine isn't running," the master mechanic said, smiling mournfully.

Meyer's car was outclassed in 1930. The retired driving star Harry Hartz had built a magnificent machine with a marvelous Miller engine and turned it over to Billy Arnold. Meyer roared into the lead and held it for the first two laps, but then Arnold drove past and began to pull farther and farther in front of the field, lap after lap.

The race became a shambles. Rickenbacker had opened the way for stock engines to compete with the pure racing engines, but few were competitive. He ordered all drivers to carry racing mechanics, which widened the cars. And he increased the starting field to forty. The track was incredibly congested.

Floyd Roberts lost control of his car on the northeast turn on the twenty-third lap, skidded and was struck by Babe Stapp's car. The cars of Deacon Litz, Marion Trexler, Johnny Seymour and Jimmy Gleason could not avoid adding to the pileup. Lou Moore walloped the wall to dodge the wreck. No one had been seriously hurt yet, but a few minutes later Cy Marshall's car careened into the wall and his brother Paul, his riding mechanic, was fatally injured.

Arnold, leading a record 198 laps, finished all by himself, some 17 minutes before runnerup Shorty Cantlon came in. Louie Schneider took third, with Meyer salvaging fourth place. Arnold was the first driver to go the distance at an average speed above 100 miles per hour, although average race speeds are rarely meaningful since they would be higher but for the slowdowns caused by accidents.

The following year, he was the fastest qualifier, but did not qualify on the first day. Arnold came from far back to take the lead on the seventh lap, and he led until the 162nd lap. Then, however, his rear axle snapped, sending the car into a wall with awful force. The right rear wheel was wrenched off and flew about two hundred feet through the air, sailing over a fence at the western edge of the grounds and striking and killing an eleven-year-old youngster playing in the front yard of his home across the street from the track. It was the most freakish accident in Speedway history.

That 1931 race was a dreadful 500 from the time a car had crashed over a wall in practice, claiming the lives of driver Joe Caccia and his mechanic, Clarence Glover. Wilbur Shaw's and Harry Butcher's cars vaulted walls, and Bill Cummings smashed into a wall in the race itself. Arnold fractured his pelvis and mechanic Spider Matlock his shoulder in their wreck. Tony Gulotta inherited the lead and in the same lap crashed right through a fence. Bill Cummings, driving relief for Spider Litz, then inherited the lead and 10 laps later walloped a wall. Lou Schneider fell into first and took a totally unexpected triumph. Sidelined early by an oil leak, Meyer watched it all from a pit wall.

"This is a very hard place," he sighed. "It is a very unforgiving place. You have to practice patience."

His patience was tested again in 1932 as he skidded close to catastrophe when his crankshaft caved in. His car was sidelined after 125 miles. Again, Arnold drove away from everyone in his Miller-Hartz, and again fate felled him. He bolted to the front on the second lap and led until the fifty-ninth circuit when he lost control on a corner and vaulted a wall again. This time his and his mechanic's injuries were reversed. He suffered a broken shoulder while Matlock suffered a broken pelvis. Discouraged, Arnold retired.

Shaw took over then and was in front with only 50 laps left when his engine went sour and he slowed and eventually was sidelined. Fred Frame, second the season before, had steadily moved up from twenty-seventh starting position. He took over the lead and eventually took the triumph.

Two practice crashes had killed one driver and one mechanic in 1932. The following year, 1933, a qualifying crash killed another driver and mechanic. Crashes in the race itself claimed two more drivers and another mechanic. Meyer said, "It is the worst part of racing, but it is a part of racing. You learn to live with death in racing. And with injuries. You always assume it will be the other fellow, not you. You feel for the other fellow, but you go on. If you weren't the sort that could go on, you wouldn't have been the sort to go into this thing in the first place."

Meyer said he was a determined driver in 1933. He admitted, "Determination doesn't mean a thing if your car can't take it, but if your car can, determination can take you to the top. Maybe it was too easy for me, winning in my first start in 1928. I was disappointed by developments the following years. I did well enough in other races, but Indy is really the race that matters. No matter how you do in other races, it's hard to win the driving title without winning Indy. That's the big bundle of points.

"You spend the year from one Indy to the next pointing for the next one. And if Indy defeats you year after year, it frustrates you. Defeat frustrates you, but breakdowns frustrate you worse. Frustration can kill your confidence and your enthusiasm. I suffered a lot of frustration for a lot of years after winning that first 500. But I was the sort who could keep up my confidence and my enthusiasm. You need determination to see you through hard times and I was a very determined young man in those days."

He did not have the best car in 1933, but he was smart enough to know it and to try to make the most of what he had. He put it to its limit, but not beyond. One after another the front-runners fell out of the lead. At 340 miles, Meyer fell into it. Shaw was second, but his car was handling badly and he was struggling with it. No one else was even close to them.

Meyer held his speed as he circled the track lap after lap, pulling away from Shaw. He passed him once, twice, three times, lapping him each time. Feeling confident, feeling for his foe, Meyer slowed as he pulled alongside Shaw to pass him for the fourth time, two laps from the finish, cupped his hands to his mouth, and hollered over the roar of the engines, "Are you going to make it?" Frustrated, Shaw refused to answer, but his riding mechanic, Billy Devore, laughed and yelled, "Sure we are." Shaw wasn't so sure, but they did, wobbling home four laps after Meyer received the checker.

"It was a cocky thing to do," Meyer admitted later, "but I didn't mean it in a mean way. I wanted to win, but I wanted Wilbur to finish."

Meyer drove his car into a celebration in Victory Lane. Now he had followed Tommy Milton as the second driver to capture this classic a second time. A microphone was shoved into his sweating, soiled face and he said, "Most drivers don't win this one even once. To have won it a second time is—well, it's a great honor. Credit to my crew. And my car."

Someone asked, "Didn't it have a driver?"

"Sure did," the driver said, grinning, and he went on to win another national title.

It had taken him five years and less than five hours to win his second Indianapolis race at a record speed of better than 104 miles per hour, but money was short during depression days and the reward was only $18,000 out of a $54,000 purse. It was the smallest payoff in fifteen years. There would be no smaller one in years to come, and in twenty-five years the payoff would be five times greater.

Looking back on it later, Meyer commented, "Money went farther in my day so you can't compare purses. But money didn't matter as much as winning. Not in a race like Indianapolis. It never has and it never will. You're a pro and you want to be paid for your performance and the risks you run and repaid for the investment you've made in money and time and effort. But you couldn't pay a man enough money to risk his neck in something if there wasn't something else in it for him. Thrills, maybe. And prestige. Pride plays a part in it.

"Win Indianapolis once and you are famous for life. There isn't much else in life like that. There are more important things, but how many great doctors or lawyers can you name by name? You know the names of the presidents maybe. Mayors or governors? No. The heavyweight champions maybe. But all the baseball champions? Or football champions? Or Olympic champions? No, win Indianapolis once and doors are open to you the rest of your life. They put that after your name all your life.

"Win it twice and you are doubly lucky and truly set apart. I started to think then of winning it a third time. No one had done that then. It would take a lot of luck. But I wanted it. I wanted the third one as much as I'd wanted the first one. I figured I might face frustration. But I maintained my determination."

That win didn't come in 1934. The field finally was cut back to thirty-three and put there permanently, although a few less started in some years owing to circumstances. Another driver and mechanic were killed in a practice crash in 1934, but traffic on the track was reduced, and while a number of cars cracked the wall, there were no further fatalities on race day. Meyer's car suffered a split oil tank, sidelining him just short of the midway mark. Frank Brisko's car collapsed in the lead just past that point. After that, Bill Cummings fought off Mauri Rose to win by 17 seconds in a duel of Miller machines.

Nor did Meyer's coveted third 500 victory come in 1935. He simply could not keep up. He kept running, but he fell far from the front. Rex Mays captured the pole at a speed of better than 120 miles per hour, but in the race his chassis failed. An outsider, Kelly Petillo, charged to the top and kept up a terrific pace. Most assumed his car would crack, but it did not. Shaw was closing in on him in the late laps, but a bit of rain near the end slowed the field for a while, and Wilbur ran out of time. Meyer went all the way, but finished far back in twelfth.

Speed-king Mays repeated on the pole in 1936 and moved to the front at first on race day, but his engine failed fast. Second twice in three 500's, the frustrated Shaw led by more than a lap at 200 miles, but his hood tore loose, he had to pit for repairs, and he was beaten by the time he got back on the track.

Driving his usual conservative, tactical race, Meyer found himself in front, with the great Ted Horn in the runnerup role. Once in the lead, Meyer was not about to let up. He held off Horn handily and won his historic third Indianapolis 500 by a wide margin as the crowd stood and cheered him.

"I can't believe it," the thirty-one-year-old Meyed admitted later. "You always think you've used up all your luck."

Some did call it a lucky triumph, for Shaw had been faster on the track, but that is often the way it is at Indianapolis. A similar situation had deprived Meyer of another win a few years before. It is a combination of car and driver that triumphs, and one can't win without the other and a little luck along the way. No one wins three at Indianapolis without being one of the best and maybe the best, and Lou Meyer's high ranking in the history of racing is assured.

He collected $31,300 of the $82,000 jackpot and additionally became the first winner to be awarded the "pace car," in this case a Packard. Previously, the pace car guided the field around at the start, then retired to be sold at an inflated price to a publicity-hungry buyer. This time, the winner took possession, grinned, and said, "I've been feeling like taking a little drive, so this comes just in time."

His historic run had consumed 3 hours and 35 minutes at an average speed of just under 110 miles per hour.

He thought he might make it four victories at Indy, but it wasn't in the cards.

After Jimmy Snyder set speed records in the time trials of 125 miles per hour for four laps and 130 for one, the 1937 classic developed into a duel between Shaw and Ralph Hepburn. The long-denied Shaw nursed a sick car home to win by a scant 2.16 seconds over Hepburn with Horn a close third. Meyer's car could not keep up with the leaders, but he finished fourth. While the 1936 event had been free of fatalities, this one wasn't. In practice, a mechanic was killed in a crash, while another car crashed into the pits, killing an engineer and a fireman.

"There does come a time when what happens in racing takes a toll on you," Meyer admitted. He no longer was hungry and his determination seemed diminished.

Meyer was not a factor up front in 1938 and retired 125 miles from the finish when his oil pump let go. Long frustrated as a driver at Indy, Lou Moore launched what would be a rewarding career as a builder by putting together a car with which Floyd Roberts could win by a wide margin over Shaw. Ernie Andres crashed in the race and his wheel flew off and fatally injured a spectator.

Meyer made one last bid for a fourth victory at Indy in 1939. It was a bitter race. Bob Swanson lost control of his car and spun in front of Roberts. Roberts' car rammed into Swanson's, cartwheeled over an outer wall, and crashed, crushing the driver. Floyd Roberts was the first former winner of the race to die at the track. Swanson was thrown onto the track. Chet Miller swerved his car to miss him, burst through a wooden barrier, and flipped upside down. Swanson was uninjured, but Miller spent six months in the hospital with his injuries.

Meanwhile, Jimmy Snyder, Meyer and Shaw dueled for the lead. Snyder led to the halfway point. Meyer moved in front with Shaw pressing him. Shaw had the faster car, a massive Maserati, but a poor pit stop dropped him more than a minute back. Nevertheless, he began to close in on the leader, cutting several seconds from his disadvantage on every lap. With only 20 miles left, Shaw caught Meyer and passed him on the homestretch heading into the first turn. Trying to wrest the lead back as they came out of the turn, Meyer accelerated too early, lost traction and skidded broadside across the track, tearing up his tires before regaining control.

Even as Meyer was pitting to replace his torn rubber, seemingly out of contention, Shaw ran out of fuel and had to pit, too. When they returned to the track, Meyer was right behind Shaw. Desperately trying to pass Shaw as they entered the second turn of the 197th lap, Meyer drove too deep into the corner and lost control of his car. The car spun completely around, rammed a wall, blew a tire and came to a stop in the infield. At that point Meyer had driven more race miles than anyone ever at Indy—5,312.

Dazed, Meyer climbed slowly from his car, took off his helmet and goggles, tossed them into the cockpit, and stood silently for a long time, watching the race rapidly run down to its conclusion. Shaw won without any pressure now, his second success at this tough track. Slowly Meyer returned to the pits. The two last skids had shaken him. "I'm getting too old for this business," he said. "It's time for me to find a safer way to earn my living."

He retired on the spot. And he found a safer way to earn his living, though remaining in racing.

The greatest engine ever raced at Indianapolis has been the Miller, created in 1921 by Harry Miller, Leo Goosen and Fred Offenhauser. Rights to the design were purchased by Offenhauser. He developed it to a point of perfection and it became known as the "Offie." In turn, rights to it were acquired by Meyer and Dale Drake, and it became the Meyer-Drake "Offie." Constantly improved, it remains the dominant power-plant in Indianapolis racing, although Ford engines defeated it several times in the late 1960's and early 1970's.

Curiously, Lou Meyer remains best-known today as an engineer whose engines won most of the 500's for many years, but it was as a racer that this cool, conservative, determined driver really made his mark at Indianapolis, a mark that remains unsurpassed.

The start of the 1971 Indianapolis 500, Al Unser (1) on his way to his second straight victory from the inside position, brother Bobby (2) outside him, pole-sitter Peter Revson behind them.

Ray Harroun on his way to victory in the inaugural Indianapolis 500, 1911.

Ready for the start of Tommy Milton's second Indianapolis victory, 1923. A crowd surrounds Milton's pole car. Alongside him are the cars of runnerup Harry Hartz, a Durant, and Dario Resta, a Packard.

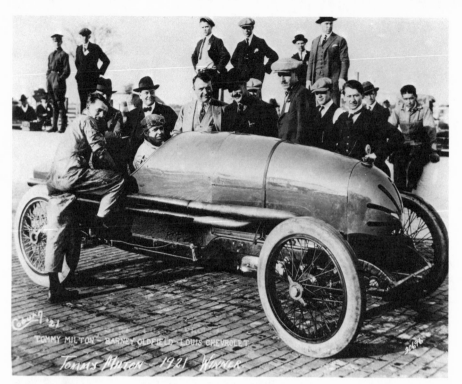

Tommy Milton in cigar-shaped 1921 winner, a Frontenac. To his left (center of photo) are Barney Oldfield and Louis Chevrolet.

Milton in 1923 winner.

Louis Meyer in his first winner, a Miller, in 1928.

Meyer and riding mechanic Lawson Harris in Louis' third winner, 1933.

Tommy Milton, 1927.

Louis Meyer, 1936.

Wilbur Shaw, 1940.

Wilbur Shaw and riding mechanic Jigger Johnson in Shaw's first winner, the Gilmore Special, in 1937.

Shaw in winning Boyle Special in 1939, a Maserati, which also won in 1940.

Above: Wilbur Shaw crashing over the wall, 1931.

Perched atop cockpit, worn-out Wilbur Shaw accepts handshake after 1939 triumph.

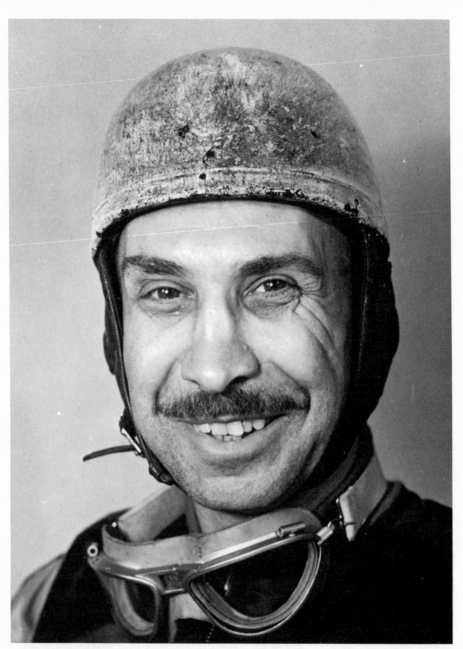

Mauri Rose, 1947.

Mauri Rose in 1947 in his Blue Crown Special which won for him in both 1947 and 1948.

Bill Vukovich in 1953 in car which carried him to 1953 and 1954 triumphs.

Borg Warner Trophy behind him, Bill Vukovich gets kissed by wife, left, and celebrity queen Marie Wilson, right, after 1953 triumph.

Smiling wife by his side, grease-smeared Vukovich sits in garage with headlined newspaper saluting his 1954 victory.

Aftermath of first-lap wreck in Foyt's first 500, 1958. Pat O'Connor was killed. The rear end of Dick Rathmann's is in rear at the right, torn off. Paul Goldsmith's 31 is at the left.

3   *Wilbur Shaw*

1937, 1939, 1940

Wilbur Shaw led Ralph Hepburn by almost two minutes with only 30 laps left in the 1937 Indianapolis 500 when, to his shock, he saw the oil gauge in the cockpit of his car drop down to the empty mark. It had been ten years since he first arrived here and he had yet to win this cruel classic. Now, within sight of victory, defeat faced him once again. "I was sick with the shock of it," he said years later. "I had tried so often and come close so often, and failed so often. . . ."

His hot engine would not run without lubrication. Without oil, it would expire or explode and he would be beaten. But the rules prohibit the addition of oil during a race. Assuming he had a little left, Shaw had no choice but to slow down and nurse his sick car as far as it would go. A smart, experienced performer, he signaled his pit crew, asking his actual lead. On his next time around, his crew held up a blackboard reading 114 seconds.

Figuring fast, Shaw calculated that he could slow by about six seconds a lap without being caught before the finish. So he slowed. And runnerup Hepburn started to close ground. It was a few laps before Hepburn, his crew, the announcer and the crowd of approximately 200,000 persons realized what was happening, but when they did bedlam broke out in The Brickyards.

No one knew exactly why Shaw was slowing, but he was. And Hepburn's crew rushed to the pit wall to wave him on excitedly. "I had given up and was settling for second until I got those signals," Hepburn recalled later. "Suddenly I knew something was wrong with Wilbur. I got excited and began to bear down."

Lap by lap, Hepburn closed in on Shaw as the fans stood and screamed. With four laps left, Hepburn emerged from the fourth turn in time to see Shaw entering the first turn. For the first time since early in the race, Hepburn had Shaw in his sights. With three laps left, Hepburn was only half the length of the straightaway behind Shaw. With two laps left, he was within a few hundred feet. And all was madness in that massive arena. As the two men entered the last lap Hepburn was within a few car lengths of the leader.

Shaw said later, "Those last 30 laps seemed to take 30 hours to run. I kept expecting the oil to give out at any second. I kept waiting for the engine to come apart. After a while, I saw Hepburn coming at me. My crew was urging me on, but I didn't dare risk running at top speed. I knew I had more speed in my car than he had in his, but I had decided not to use it until I had to. When he caught me, I had to." As they thundered through the short chute between the third and fourth turns, Hepburn caught Shaw. As they roared out of the fourth turn, Hepburn pulled his car alongside Shaw's and nosed ahead.

Shaw punched the accelerator and his car leaped back into the lead and surged down the stretch in front as the fans hollered excitedly. Shaw flashed across the finish line under the waving checkered flag, then Hepburn came across, just 2.16 seconds later, which endures to this day as the closest finish in the history of the speedway marathon.

As Shaw eased off the throttle and coasted through the rest of the stretch, his engine started to make a rattling sound. "There was no oil left. My car would have been dead before I could race another lap," he laughed later. He drove into Victory Lane, triumphant in this prestigious test for the first time, smiling broadly as the photographers' bulbs popped in his face, and he said, "I was a little lucky today, gentlemen." And Ralph Hepburn pulled his car into the pits, stopped, and buried his head in his hands.

Wilbur Shaw may have been born to be a racer. He was born in 1902 in Shelbyville, Indiana, not far from Indianapolis, and surrounded by smaller racetracks. He grew up reading racing headlines and sneaking into tracks. His father was a happy-go-lucky wanderer who left his family while Wilbur was but a boy. Wilbur was reared by his mother in cities around the state and eventually in Indianapolis, itself. While in high school, he installed batteries in the new Stutz cars. Then he went to work for a battery firm that provided power for electric cars. Finally, he landed a job with a man who built gasoline-powered cars and racers.

In his spare time, the youngster built his own race car out of junk parts on the second floor of a warehouse. Once he had finished it, he had to figure out how to get it outside. He knocked out a window, built a ramp and lowered the car down it, almost wrecking the creation in the process. He took his car to a half-mile dirt track on the outskirts of Indianapolis, put it on the oval during a practice period prior to a race, and within two laps had been told to take his "junker" somewhere else. He took it to the track at Lafayette, where he raced it. He went too fast for his skills and the car's capacity, skidded, rolled over and wrecked the car beyond repair. "In thirty seconds, I had wiped out six months of the toughest kind of work," he mourned later.

He did not give up, however. He haunted the racetracks, begging rides. Older drivers got their kicks by having him hang on to the tail of their racer while they practiced, driving wildly in an attempt to throw him off. His courage convinced others he deserved rides. Owners of bad cars without good drivers gave him some chances. Without winning, he was sufficiently impressive to begin to get better rides. He began to win races, making the most of his opportunities, moving up. By the middle 1920's, Wilbur Shaw was making a name for himself. By 1927, he had found a sponsor, Fritz Holliday, who would buy and back a car in which he could compete in the Indianapolis 500.

The best car they could get was the one that had carried Jimmy Murphy to his death at Syracuse three years earlier. It had been rebuilt, and Lou Meyer, who had helped, came with it from California as a mechanic. The car was named "The Jynx Special," after a tire company that put money into the project. The car ran rough and Meyer was moved in to relieve Shaw for 125 miles at midrace. Shaw returned to finish fourth after better cars had broken down. It was a good debut for the twenty-four-year-old youngster and convinced him he could make a mark in the game.

"It was a thrill just being there," he said later. "I was awed to be among men who had become my idols. I was unnerved by the race itself. I felt I had been sucked into a hundred-mile-an-hour tornado. I was never so scared in my life. Once I got used to it, I lost my fear. I learned I could drive with the best of them. I just needed a car that could compete. I couldn't wait for the next race. For me, Memorial Day at Indy was my birthday, Christmas, and all the good days of the year rolled into one. I loved that race. It became my life."

It was not all of his life, and it was not an easy life. He had gotten married, and while he was racing on the circuit that summer his young wife and her infant died in childbirth. Trying to forget his loss, he resumed racing. In a fling at the land-speed record on the Daytona sands in Florida, his car caught fire and he drove it into the ocean to extinguish the flames much as Tommy Milton had done some years earlier. Malcolm Campbell captured the new standard at better than 206 miles per hour. Frank Lockhart crashed and was killed trying to top it.

Shaw returned to Indianapolis to drive a new car for Phil Shafer, a new backer. When expected sponsorship help fell through, however, the car was put up for sale. While Shaw was trying to find another backer, Lou Meyer found one, who bought the car. While Meyer was putting the mighty new Miller into the starting field, Shaw was climbing into a rebuilt wreck and qualifying it on race day. While Meyer was winning the race, Shaw was watching after having been sidelined by engine failure a little more than 100 miles along.

Discouraged, Shaw and other drivers who had been having trouble landing top rides on the title trail withdrew from membership in the sponsoring American Automobile Association and competed on unsanctioned "outlaw" tracks which gave them a better break. When, however, they were barred from the 1929 Indianapolis race, Shaw and others sought and received reinstatement.

Wilbur had fallen in love again and remarried. He began to win 100-milers. On the day Ray Keech won the 1929 Indianapolis 500 in Indiana, Shaw won the Bridgeville 100 in Pennsylvania. Winning the Syracuse 100 in record time earned him an offer of a good ride in Chicagoan Mike Boyle's car at Altoona. Wilbur was winning until escaping fuel fumes almost asphyxiated him. He had to be helped from his car and hospitalized. Meyer won, and with the victory was on his way to the first of his two straight national driving titles. His duel for dominance with Shaw started to really heat up.

Shaw returned to Indianapolis for the 1930 race, but the bulky car provided him rode raggedly and a new Miller engine failed at 135 miles. When Wilbur got an offer from Johnny Vance to compete in California, he jumped at it, picked his new car up in Daytona and drove it west with a young hopeful, Mauri Rose, hitching a ride to the coast. The car wasn't competitive, however, and Shaw shifted into another man's mount. He walloped a wall with this one, cracking ribs and earning a rest in the hospital.

Wilbur was a wild one at this time in his career, jumping from sponsor to sponsor, driving cars so hard they broke, gypsying across the country. He had daring and ability, but lacked good equipment and sometimes seemed to lack good sense.

The Duesenberg brothers, Fred and Augie, had split up. Shaw spent the winter working in Augie's shop, helping prepare a racer for the 1931 Indy, only to have the engine come apart during time trials there. Shaw switched to one of Fred's cars, which driver Phil Pardee disliked. Pardee had qualified it, so had to start the race in it. However, after the first lap, Shaw was free to jump into the driver's seat, alongside the riding mechanic.

Shaw never had sat in the cockpit, much less driven the car. The cockpit turned out to be so big he was almost lost in it. And the ride in the big Dusie was so smooth he did not realize he was going as fast as he was. Trying to pass four cars in rapid succession on the sixtieth lap, Shaw ran out of straightaway, found himself too deep into a turn, lost traction trying to cut across the corner, skidded sideways, vaulted an outer wall, sailed thirty feet through some telephone wires, and landed upright and all right outside the oval.

Those who saw Shaw's car careen out of control over the wall and heard the horrifying crash could not believe he and his mechanic had not been badly hurt or killed, but they were not. In fact, when Wilbur returned to his pits, skinned up, but bandaged, Fred Duesenberg ordered him to drive relief in the team's sister car and called driver Jimmy Gleason in. Gleason came in and Shaw went out. As he accelerated, he found in front of him three of the four cars he had been passing when he went over the wall a few laps earlier.

As Shaw recalled it—and it was his favorite story—as he went past Phil Shafer, Shorty Cantlon and Ralph Hepburn, each in turn seemed to do a double-take, then slowed sharply. "They must have thought they were seeing a ghost," he explained. "Except for the almost identical numbers, 32 and 33, the two Duesenbergs *were* identical."

Shaw was so busy passing cars and wondering why they were

giving him so much room to get by that he again ran out of straightaway and heard the tires squeal as he went sideways. Wrestling the wheel desperately, he managed to straighten out this time, missing the wall by an inch or so.

Hepburn admitted later, "I thought I was seeing the same accident twice in a row, as though in a dream . . . or a nightmare. It unnerved me, I must admit."

It unnerved Shaw, too. He slowed his speed to a reasonable rate. First place was far out of reach, anyway. Shaw drove steadily the rest of the way until he turned the car back to Gleason for the final laps. They settled for sixth place, well back of winner Schneider. The rest of the year Shaw's cars ran into one mechanical problem after another as he toured the remainder of the championship trail, then continued on to the Far West for winter racing.

In California he finally found a car which would hold together for 100 laps, and with it he won his first important triumph on the West Coast, whipping Wild Bill Cummings in a close finish on the dirt at Ascot Park, outside of L.A. Impressed, a sponsor offered Shaw a new Miller car. He grabbed it and with it won two of the next three Ascot features, then went to Muroc Dry Lake and set a speed record for cars of its class.

As a prize, Shaw was presented a metal "crash helmet" that had been worn by England's famous H.O.D. Segrave when he became the first man to drive a car at better than 200 miles-per-hour. Shaw took a lot of ribbing about his hard hat, which was without a visor and looked like an upside-down mug. But he wore it in races, and within a few years all were wearing something like it. Up until that time, drivers wore cloth "aviator" caps, which buckled under the chin, but provided no protection from a blow to the head.

Despite this concession to safety, Shaw was ruggedly old-fashioned in some ways and refused to wear a seat belt because it kept him erect and prevented him from ducking deep into the cockpit as he preferred to do when a crash was coming.

Ralph Hepburn crashed at Oakland in January, which removed

him from the 1932 Indianapolis field and gave Shaw a start in
Ralph's rebuilt racer. Engine problems cost Shaw a high starting
position and slowed him in the early stages of the race, but when
Billy Arnold and other front-runners crashed or failed in the first
half of the event, Shaw found himself in front in the 500 for the
first time.

"I was the happiest guy in the world," he recalled later. However, the engine was sick and he had a hard time staying ahead of
Fred Frame. Finally, with a little more than 100 miles left, the
engine died during a pit stop and Frame went on to win. Shaw's
happiness died with the engine. "It was a blue Monday," he
mourned.

Shaw was badly banged up in two accidents in California that
winter and in between made a fruitless boat trip to Italy for a race
at Monza. On his return he did some stunt driving for a Jimmy
Cagney movie, *The Crowd Roars*, which still shows on late-night
television. The director, Howard Hawks, decided to back Wilbur
in a new car project for the Indianapolis renewal. But this was in
the depths of the depression and after President Roosevelt closed
the banks, Hawks withdrew from the project.

Money was in short supply and Speedway president Rickenbacker cut the 500 purse sharply, but did not discontinue his event
as other track operators did.

Shaw shifted into Leon Duray's car for the 1933 race, which
was almost canceled, anyway. After the physical examinations
required of each driver, a top contender, Howdy Wilcox, was de-
clared out with a diabetic condition. That was the morning of the
race and Shaw helped circulate a petition signed by all the drivers
to the effect that if Wilcox was not restored to the race, the other
drivers would not drive. Rickenbacker refused to relent, rather
than risk an accident caused by a sick competitor. He threatened to
run the race if he had to drive the only car in it himself. The drivers
backed down and the race was run with Wilcox's car starting at the
rear with Mauri Rose substituting in the cockpit.

Shaw's mount bucked like a bronco across the bricks, but after the good cars caved in, Wilbur found only Lou Meyer in front of him. But there was no way Shaw could keep up with Meyer's car. Shaw was lapped repeatedly by Meyer, who rubbed salt into Wilbur's wounds by hollering over to ask if he could finish the last time he passed. Under the circumstances, Shaw was satisfied to finish second, four laps after Lou Meyer moved across for his second 500 success. However, Wilbur's frustration was mounting by now. He went on to win a big race at Milwaukee in mid-July, but Meyer went on to win his third national title. "Meyer is the man to beat," Shaw said. Their rivalry was getting hot.

Shaw went into the Wilcox car for the 1934 Indy 500 and qualified it second fastest in the field at above 117 miles per hour. He was second in the early stages of the race, but within 50 miles the oil plug had worked loose, dumped the oil out, and aborted another bid. Desperate to drive, Shaw grabbed an opportunity to relieve Lou Moore for almost 200 miles in midrace, moving the car from sixth to fourth. It finished third. Then Shaw went into Mauri Rose's pits and was ready to relieve him, but the weary Rose refused to surrender and finished second. Wild Bill Cummings came in first.

It is a dangerous thing to do, driving in a high-speed race a car you have not driven before, and some drivers would not do it, but Shaw was daring. Like Lou Meyer, Shaw was determined and able. But unlike Lou, Wilbur had little to show for his daring determination and driving ability after five 500's. To cut congestion on the track, the field had been cut to thirty-three starters, and much of the brick course had been paved over to improve the racing surface, but fatalities and serious injuries were frequent in these years, and they bothered even the bravest of men.

"You had to accept it without thinking about it. When you started to think too much about it it was time to quit," Shaw said. "If you were the sort of person who worried about it, you weren't the sort to be in racing in the first place.

"I guess the only real reason to be in racing is if you can win races, however. The risks you run are too great if the rewards aren't great. And I wasn't winning much in those days. But I always thought I would win. No matter how many ways I found to lose, I always thought I would win. I had the sort of ego all good athletes have to have if they're going to be the best. I thought I was the best, not second-best or tenth-best, but the best, and I believed only bad breaks beat me."

He had been second-best in 1933 and he was second-best again in 1935. He found a backer who would finance him in building an Indianapolis car that year, and he built a beautiful car. But he could not catch Kelly Petillo's car with a closing surge that was slowed by rain in the late laps. Shaw had fallen behind early in the event. During a pit stop he had been handed a bottle of milk to drink for refreshment. Afraid of breaking glass in the pits, he did not know what to do with the bottle when he was waved away. Hesitating, he let his engine die. He hurled the bottle away, but before he was restarted he had lost the race.

"It seemed like something always was coming up to keep me from finishing first," he sighed. "I began to believe I was jinxed."

However, he persisted. For Shaw, speed was his life. Along with such members of the Hollywood set as Jimmy Stewart, Henry Fonda and Brian Aherne, he learned to fly airplanes. He raced planes and motorboats as well as cars. He even made parachute jumps from planes. For a while he had a piece of the Los Angeles Aircraft Company, which he sold in order to own his own operation in racing for 1936.

Working with limited money and a little sponsorship support, in a day when an independent could invade Indianapolis on a shoestring, Shaw again constructed his own car. But, in doing so, he ran a drill into his hand, severing an artery and almost bleeding to death before being hospitalized.

While Shaw's hand was healing, an aide had to do the detail work on the car. The hood was not put on properly. This was not discovered until well into the 500 itself, months later. Shaw and his car were outclassing the field. In front by 80 seconds at 200 miles, Wilbur was counting his winnings when suddenly the hood tore loose. It took 17 minutes in the pits to put it back on properly. By that time, Meyer was on his way to becoming the first three-time winner in the history of the great race. Shaw spent four minutes less time on the track than the winner, but Wilbur was a loser once again. Shaw sarcastically turned on his errant aide and stormed off. "I was low," he recalled later.

But he went on. Motor racing is a sport in which the good ones go on. Sometimes it takes a long time for the good ones to get to the top. Somehow, some never got there. Wilbur Shaw got there in 1937 at the age of thirty-five after ten years of trying at Indianapolis. He endured a difficult off-season. He almost lost some of his vision when his goggles were shattered in a dirt-track melee. Splinters of glass imbedded in an eye and had to be dug out. He was almost impaled on his steering wheel when he rammed a barrier in another accident.

He rebuilt his wrecked racer himself, and was broke by the time he got to Indy. In the 10-lap, 25-mile time trial of that day he set a new speed record of better than 122 miles per hour. Preparing his car in the pits a few days later, he missed death when an out-of-control racer narrowly missed him and plowed into the car in front of him and the men around it, killing two of them. Years later, Shaw admitted, "I can still close my eyes and see every detail of that crash exactly as it happened."

On race day his aides discovered they lacked the right refueling gauge in the pits and rushed ten miles from the track to return with the proper piece ten minutes before the race was to begin. In the race Shaw shot into the lead at the 65-mile mark and found he had by far the fastest car. It was a brutally hot day and most drivers required relief. Ralph Hepburn got relief from Bob Swanson for 60 miles, but Wilbur went on. Shaw's right foot was being burned by hot metal floorboards, but he was two minutes ahead of

Hepburn with 75 miles left when he started to run out of oil.

It was then that he smartly calculated the reduced speed he could risk to conserve his remaining oil, over the last 30 laps, yet stay ahead of the runnerup. His slowdown tactics took him to the last lap in the lead, when Hepburn caught him, only to have Shaw shoot back in front with a final surge that carried him across the finish line with, at last, his first triumph at this cruel oval. "A lot of things went wrong as usual, but we won this one for a change," he sighed. "I guess when it's your day, it's your day."

Shaw was so exhausted he had to be helped out of his car. He could not stand up. His right foot had been roasted and required treatment. He had lost ten pounds. It had taken him 4 hours, 24 minutes and 7 seconds at a record average speed of 113 miles per hour to win by two seconds, the closest contest in the history of the classic. While everyone else celebrated, his wife tucked him in bed. He lay there unable to sleep, in agony over his raw foot. Finally, a friend brought him a handful of sleeping pills which put him out.

He collected more than $35,000. The money meant that he could go first class in racing for a while. And he wanted to go on. "Winning one, I wanted to win another one. The money I made gave me a good chance to win another one. But the money meant nothing compared to the pride I felt at finally having beaten this hard place. I was champion of Indy. I had worked and waited so long, it took a long time for it to sink in. The frustration and pain I'd put up with faded after I finished first. That's what racing is, finishing first," he said.

With Indy's big bundle of points in his pocket, Wilbur went on to finish first in the race for the national driving title. Along the way he was impressed by the powerful foreign cars he faced in an international race on Long Island. A sponsor agreed to buy him a new Maserati from Italy. However, when it arrived it turned out to have been assembled with too small an engine to produce the speeds necessary to win at Indianapolis. Shaw turned the car over to Mauri Rose and returned to his old car.

Many of the new cars could go faster. Shaw set a steady pace of 115 miles per hour in the 1938 Indy while faster cars fell out in front of him, but he was two laps short of Floyd Roberts, who did not fall out. Shaw settled for his third second-place finish in the 500, Rose pushed the underpowered Maserati into fifth place before he pushed it too hard and it failed.

The Maserati was returned to Italy to be rebuilt with a bigger engine for 1939. It was returned with a bigger engine, but with cracked cylinder blocks. New blocks had to be ordered and shipped out. By the time these came and were installed, a starting problem developed. When this was solved, an oil leak developed. This was corrected just in time for the 500. But in the race the car worked. Jimmy Snyder captured the pole with a new record speed of 130 miles per hour, but Shaw finished on the front row at close to 129. Meyer placed in between the two. And the race swiftly became a three-way battle between them.

The race was a rough one. Just past the halfway point Bob Swanson careened out of control coming out of turn two, triggering a multicar crackup that killed defending champion Floyd Roberts. Shaw was told of Roberts' death during a pit stop and it hit him hard.

The pit stop almost cost him the race. His refueling equipment fouled up. Meyer was in and out of the pits a full minute faster, building up a big lead. With 180 miles to go, Shaw set out to catch Meyer. Moving his massive Maserati on the ragged edge of losing control, Shaw cut a second or more from Meyer's lead on every lap, lap after lap, in a dogged pursuit. With 100 miles left, he was within half a minute. With 20 miles left, Shaw caught up. The crowd, caught up in the madness of the moment, came to its feet in excitement.

Coming off the fourth corner, Shaw accelerated ahead of Meyer as they moved into the mainstretch. Coming into the first turn,

Meyer accelerated, trying to wrest back the lead. He lost control, skidding sideways before righting his car just short of the wall. Having torn his tires up, Meyer had to move back into the pits. When he returned to the track, he was well back.

At this point, however, Shaw's fuel supply started to run out. Within sight of victory, Wilbur had to risk pitting again. He darted into his pits, a few gallons of fuel were dumped into his tanks, and he darted out again. This time, Meyer was right behind him. Three laps from the finish, Meyer made a last bid to top Shaw. He drove deep into the second corner, too deep, slid again, spun, struck the wall, blew a tire and skidded to a stop in the infield.

Shaw drove into Victory Lane at Indianapolis for the second time even as Meyer was announcing his retirement. "No competitor ever reached the end of the championship trail with greater fighting spirit," admitted an admiring Shaw of Meyer.

Shaw collected more than $27,000 for his victory. He formed his own company to market films of the Indianapolis event. He took a job representing Firestone and toured the country giving, of all things, speeches on highway safety. He continued on tour, winning enough points for his second national title. The mustachioed Shaw was a popular champion.

His great goal now was to become the first man ever to win at Indianapolis twice in a row and with this to match Meyer's mark of three 500 crowns. Shaw's Maserati had been the first foreign-made car to capture the classic in twenty years, and it inspired the first full-fledged foreign invasion of the Speedway in many years.

The Italian factory was making a more powerful Maserati and Wilbur wanted one for the 1940 race, but he was not sure it would meet the specifications for entrants, so he stuck with his winner. Raul Riganti did drive one in the race, but hit the wall with it within 60 miles. Frenchmen Rene Dreyfus and Rene Lebegue drove other Maseratis at Indianapolis, but one was broken in practice and the other was soundly whipped in the race, finishing eight laps back.

It was not merely the Maserati, but the driver—an experienced, skilled Shaw, far from his undependable days—that took the checker at Indy. Only the Rex Mays car, formerly Meyer's car, was faster. Shaw and Mays both qualified at above 127 miles per hour for the 1940 race, with Mays moving onto the pole by a fraction of a second. And Mays did move in front at the start. But Shaw cut him down at 85 miles and began to pull away.

Shaw was 40 seconds in front at 185 miles when he made the first of his two planned pit stops. Here, his engine died. "I almost died," Shaw said later. Chief mechanic Cotton Henning tried desperately to crank it up but failed five or six times. He ducked into the cockpit to check the ignition switch. An aide tried the crank. The engine came to life! Shaw shoved the clutch out and took off, flooring Henning and running over his foot with a rear wheel as he roared back toward the track.

Mays, Mauri Rose, Ted Horn and Joe Thorne had passed Shaw and he had fallen to fifth. Dark clouds were convening overhead ominously. The threat of rain, which could curtail the race, hung over the drivers. It was an official race once it passed the halfway point, and the order would stand if the race was stopped. Shaw shot around the course in the gathering gloom in a desperate attempt to take the lead back before rain ruined his dream. The others had pit stops scheduled around the midway mark. Shaw closed ground on them, lap after lap. They went into the pits, one after another. Shaw found himself in front again.

But Shaw had another pit stop to make. According to his crew's calculations he could not make it past 350 to 360 miles without a second refueling. With the black clouds increasing in the skies and a damp wind blowing across the course, he did not dare surrender the lead at any time. Determined to build up a big lead prior to his last pit stop, Shaw pressed his great car to its limits, hurtling around the oval daringly. For 40 laps he picked up a second or two on every lap. He drove right to the 360-mile mark before ducking into the pits for fuel.

He was in and out in a hurry, still leading. Determinedly, he set out to increase his advantage again. But even as he did so, lightning cut through the skies. Eight laps later, rain began to fall and the yellow signals came out. The last 120 miles were run under caution at reduced speed, Shaw comfortably in front, worried only that something would snap under him, waiting for the checkered flag to be flown in his face. When he won it was worth $31,000 in gold to him at its prewar value and a great deal of glory, which meant even more to him. "After years of frustration, I finally was all alone at the top," the thirty-eight-year-old veteran sighed.

He had finished first three times and second twice in an eight-year stretch. No one had humbled this place in this way previously. Having become the first to win two in a row here and the second to win three in a career, he wanted now to make it three straight and become the first to win four. Despite the uncertainties of racing, he was regarded as a good bet to do it. He was the best driver at the big track and he had the best car in competition. It had held up through two hard races. If the car could last one more, the driver could conquer all.

Shaw took an increased role with the Firestone Company, and he and his wife settled in Akron, Ohio, to be near the home office. Content and comfortable, he cut his racing schedule so drastically he really did not defend his national title, allowing Rex Mays to capture the crown for the third time. On the short tracks, Rex was king. But on the big track, Wilbur was the boss. When he returned to Indy in May of 1941, Shaw was confident to the point of cockiness.

Mauri Rose captured the pole position at 128 miles per hour. Three-time pole-sitter Mays was second fastest, fractionally short. Shaw was third fastest, comfortably set to start on the outside of the front row. As race day approached, all proceeded smoothly.

Then, a few days before the race, Shaw's old driving shoes were stolen from his garage. They were well worn and beat up. Their loss might have been meaningless. But Shaw was superstitious about such things. He had worn the shoes in every race he'd run for years, and he worried about their loss.

"A friend found me an old pair much like them to replace them, but they weren't the real ones," Shaw said years later. "I had a premonition of bad luck and couldn't shake it. I suppose I was being foolish—not the way it worked out, however."

Race morning, as he was showering at the home of a friend near the track, he heard fire engines in the distance. He instantly thought about the possibility of a fire in the garage area at the Speedway, an ancient area full of fuel. His friend rushed to tell him that it was, indeed, the garage area that was aflame. Shaw dressed and rushed to the track. The area was a shambles. Fuel drums were exploding and flames were shooting into the air. The teams were pushing their cars to safety and salvaging what equipment they could, even as firemen fought the inferno.

Shaw was relieved to find his team had been on hand and had gotten their car and most of their equipment out of the area. Before the fire was put out, three cars were destroyed, but only one that had been scheduled to start in the race. However, much equipment was destroyed or damaged. Shaw's equipment seemed in good shape. The only thing that worried him was that the fire hoses had washed away the chalked markings on his tires. He always balanced his own tires and had marked one not to be used because he could not balance it properly. He could not figure out which one this was before he had to take to the track.

The traditional command, "Gentlemen, start your engines," was given to the cars one hour late. Shaw's car would not start. Desperately, Henning cranked it again and again. Desperately the crew started to push it as Shaw pressed on the accelerator. The rest of the field was already away, settling into their starting positions on the parade lap. In a few seconds, Shaw's car would have to be pushed aside, and his dream race would be done. Suddenly, the car started. Relieved, Shaw roared onto the track, overhauled the field, and slipped into his starting slot. The green flag flew, and they were off.

Most of the race was run as Wilbur wanted it. In the early stages he had to duel Mays and Rose for the lead, but after 45 laps the lead was his. His stronger car started to pull away from the pack. After he made his second scheduled pit stop, he led by 80 seconds with 150 miles left. He was confident as he circled the course, easily lapping other cars. His easiest triumph seemed certain.

Suddenly, as he headed down the homestretch on his 152nd lap, his car swayed. "It was," he said "as if a sudden gust of wind had given the tail a little push." As he drove into the first turn, the right rear wheel bent, the car's rear end swung out and the car looped into the wall, bounced off, spun around and hammered the barrier a second time with brutal force before coming to a stop. "It was," he said, "as if someone or something had simply shoved me across the track."

Had the unbalanced tire been used? Shaw never knew for sure. No one ever will know. But the spokes of the wheel had broken as if an unbalanced tire had put too severe a strain on it. In any event, his day was done. The victory that might have been his fourth went to Mauri Rose, driving relief after his own car failed. Mays was second for the second straight year. Rose, too, would go on to take the checker at Indy three times, but Mays would never take it.

Well, Wilbur Shaw had won it three times. No one ever has won it more times. Shaw might have, but he did not. He finished second twice when he might have finished first, and the fates felled him in 1941 when he might have finished first one last time. He was not to have another try. He had endured his last mile at Indy, more than Meyer or any other man to that time—5,392 miles. It remains today among the five top totals of all time. And he had led for 508 laps. Ralph DePalma had led for 613 laps. These endure as the two top totals of all time.

When time ran out on Wilbur Shaw in 1941, he was paralyzed from the waist down from a blow his spine had absorbed in the impact of walloping the wall twice. But within weeks his worst fears faded. He started to recover and began to plot another 500 victory. Within the year, however, the United States was drawn into World War II and the Speedway was shuttered for four years. He never raced again.

Shaw worked at aircraft construction through the war, often flying supplies across the country. The Speedway was offered to the military but refused. It lay unused through the war, until early in 1945 when Shaw drove there one final time, all alone, testing a new tire. He was deeply disturbed to find the track in total disrepair. The surface of the oval was cracked. Grass grew between the bricks on the straightaway. The wooden grandstands were rotting away. It looked like "an abandoned farm," he said.

The war ended that year, but Rickenbacker wanted to devote himself to his Eastern Air Lines. He did not want to raise the money necessary to get the track back in shape. He was willing to sell the real estate for a housing development. This country's classic course was in danger when Wilbur Shaw stepped in. "The world's last great speed shrine must be preserved at any cost," he said.

Sentimentally, Rickenbacker offered to sell Shaw the place for the money he had put into it. This figured out to about $750,000. But more would be needed for repairs. Wilbur went to a bank to borrow money. He went to individual investors to get pledges of $25,000 apiece. He still fell short. Friends suggested some wealthy individuals who might wish to take over the project. Reluctant to lose control of the oval personally, Shaw sought out Terre Haute businessman Anton "Tony" Hulman only when time was running out on his hopes of saving the Speedway.

Hulman, a devoted Hoosier, a former athlete, and a car-racing enthusiast, who had not missed seeing the 500 since 1914, agreed to take over the track in time for racing to be resumed in 1946. "I don't care whether I make money on it or not. This is the greatest sporting event in the state, if not in the world, and I want to see it grow even greater," Hulman pledged.

On an investment of approximately $1 million, Tony Hulman became chairman of the board and majority stockholder of the

Indianapolis Speedway, while Wilbur Shaw became president and general manager.

True to his pledge, Hulman has plowed profits into modernizing improvements annually ever since. While no attendance or gate-receipt figures are announced, taxes are heavy, and it is generally agreed that the track has meant more to him in personal satisfaction than in profit.

The Indianapolis Speedway became a cornerstone on which a network of super racing courses has been built across the country, the one above all others which is financially solid, luring a million paying patrons in the month of May and grossing close to $10 million in the only month it is used except for tests. Hulman's modest initial investment now is worth many millions. His track has endured to continue a tradition which sets its classic contest above all other sporting events.

Wilbur Shaw presided over the Speedway through a time in which it began its greatest growth, a time when Mauri Rose became the second man ever to win the 500 two years in a row and the third ever to take the checkered flag for a third time.

Shaw was preparing for his tenth race as president, one in which Bill Vukovich, the third driver to win the event two years running, was to bid to become the fourth to win it a third time, when death took Wilbur shortly before it took Bill.

In October of 1954, returning from a test drive at a Chrysler proving grounds in Michigan, Shaw was a passenger in a single-engine private plane. In icing, snowing, freezing weather conditions enroute back to Indianapolis the plane crashed in a cornfield near Decatur, Indiana, killing all aboard.

The following May, Bill Vukovich crashed and was killed while leading the Indianapolis 500 in quest of his third straight triumph there.

4 Mauri Rose

1941,* 1947, 1948

When Mauri Rose crossed the finish line in the 1941 Indy 500 it was one of the most surprising victories in the history of the classic and it remains an almost unique triumph to this day.

Rose was a good driver, but good days had eluded him at this track. He had come close to conquering it a couple of times, but had fallen short. In his ninth try he captured the pole position, but then he broke down with engine failure at 150 miles and was seemingly finished for the day.

Mauri had driven one of two cars entered by Lou Moore. When Mauri told Moore he was going to go through pit row to see if any team might need him as a relief driver, Moore said, "The hell you are! If you're ready to go again, I'll call in Davis and you can finish the race in his car."

Floyd Davis was driving the team's sister car. He had not driven it well. He had qualified it only seventeenth fastest, some seven miles per hour slower than first-fastest Rose. At this point in the race, he was running in twelfth place, while Rose had been contending for first place when his car quit on him.

"There's nothing wrong with the car that a little more pressure

* Shared the victory, winning in relief of Floyd Davis.

61

on the throttle won't cure," Moore told Rose. Mauri shrugged and
agreed to give it a go, but he suggested Moore wait to call Davis
in until the car was due for refueling. Moore agreed, and at 180
miles motioned Davis in and, when he got in, ordered him out of
the cockpit. This was the fourth and final 500 Davis drove. Dis-
gusted, he quit.

Mauri moved out onto the track two minutes behind the leaders.
He admitted later, "At that point I had no thought of winning, but
I thought I could pick up some positions and make some money.
You never know who's going to get into trouble ahead of you. I
had nothing to lose by letting it all out. So I drove as hard as I
could. It was a good car and it went good. Some cars fell out in
front of me and I passed others. In time, I realized I was in contention for the top spot. Then I really got interested and really bore
down."

Rose went from twelfth to tenth in his first 50 miles, and at the
midway mark in the event, just 20 miles later, was seventh. He
passed Chet Miller, Ralph Hepburn, Ted Horn and Rex Mays in
the next 100 miles and was third with 150 miles left. There was no
way he could have caught Wilbur Shaw, but he was closing in on
runnerup Cliff Bergere when Shaw's wheel bent and his car was
hung on a wall with 125 miles to go.

Shortly after Shaw's Maserati was towed away and the track
was cleared, the green flag flew again. Rose drove past Bergere and
into the lead. From there, Rose pulled steadily away from the field,
finishing more than a lap in front. The first gasoline-fueled car to
go the distance without a single pit stop, Bergere's mount was
weakening near the end and he was passed by Mays, Horn and
Hepburn in the last laps.

Bergere was not a winner, but he was steady. He kept his cars
going more miles of 500's than any other driver—more than
6,142 miles. Until A. J. Foyt surpassed them more than a quarter-
century later, Bergere and Chet Miller had driven more Indy
classics than any other drivers—sixteen. These were not consecu-

tive. Until Foyt bettered it, Rose held the record with fifteen straight starts at the Speedway. But the best Bergere ever did was third place two times. Rose went on to finish in first place three times.

Rose's victory in 1941 was his first. Although he has to share honors with Floyd Davis for this one, he is generally listed as one of the four three-time winners in the history of Indianapolis. Certainly, there can be no question of his stature, as he went on to win two more as a soloist following World War II, though even one of these is tainted.

In 1941 everyone expected Wilbur Shaw to become the first four-time winner of the 500 with his third straight triumph, but when he crashed out of it while far in front, he opened the door to Mauri Rose. Rose went through it to become one of only eight men to win this classic contest more than once, and he has been one of only two drivers ever to win it in relief of another.

Rose's success in the last 500 prior to the war was stunning because he had shown only occasional flashes of winning form previously. He was in his ninth Indianapolis race and for his first starts had few impressive performances. However, he was a smart, skilled and confident driver who needed only good cars to be among the best.

"You can't carry your car across the finish line first," he once said. "You can't separate the car and the driver. Both are important. But the best car won't win with a bad driver and the best driver won't win with a bad car. A good car can help a driver. A good driver can help a car. I was a good driver, but it was a while before I got good cars. How good I was I don't know. Some good drivers never get a good car. We'll never know how good they might have been."

Rose was out of Columbus, Ohio, a short, slight man, who wore a long, thick mustache. Off the track he constantly smoked a pipe. He looked like anything but a race driver. But, then, a lot of race drivers don't look the way we assume they should. They come in all shapes and sizes. And all sorts of temperaments. Some are extroverted, some introverted. Some are loud, some quiet. All share an ability to do this thing without wondering why they dare do it, but some are more confident in their talent than others.

Rose was always soft-spoken and reserved in public, but in the fraternity of racers, he radiated confidence consistently. He was just beginning to break into the big time when he hitched a ride west with Wilbur Shaw in 1930. Shaw already had driven Indy three times and was recognized as a "comer." Rose, apparently, wanted to impress him.

As Shaw recalls it, they talked racing as they rode across country, but Rose spoke mainly of "what a wonderful driver he was." As Shaw said later, "According to him, no one else knew half as much about racing as he did." Shaw said, "This was particularly irritating to me because I was equally certain I was the best in the business."

Shaw later admitted he never met a top performer who did not believe he was the best, but most managed to restrain themselves in speaking publicly of their skills. At the time Shaw was so annoyed he'd just as soon not have seen Mauri again. Later, however, he confessed he was impressed when Rose began to back up his boasts.

"It wasn't all up front. He had something behind it, too. He really knew how to race," Shaw said. Soon, when Wilbur had an extra car, he turned it over to Mauri. "I always knew Rose would give me my money's worth," he said.

Mauri did not have many good cars in his first years at Indy, but he did get a break to get into the starting field for the first time. This was in 1933. Mauri's struggle to qualify a mediocre car ended when the beast broke down on the final afternoon of time trials. Disappointed, he decided to stay around to see the race. However, he had impressed the owner of Howdy Wilcox's car. When Wilcox was disqualified on race morning because of a diabetic condition, Rose was offered and accepted the role as substitute.

The drivers protested Wilcox's disqualification, not Rose's substitution. But because Rose was a rookie who had never driven so much as a single lap either in the race or in the Wilcox car, he was moved from the front row back to the forty-second and last starting position after the drivers relented and agreed to race. "I knew I had no chance from that far back, but I was willing to take my opportunity just to break into the race," Rose recalled later.

When his engine failed at 120 miles, he was finished, but not before he had made a marvelous move into fourth place.

"I could have won with that car. I could have won from up front for sure. So could Howdy have. I could even have won from way back where I started if the engine had held up, but I had to push her awful hard to have any chance at all," Mauri mourned later. No car ever again started from so far back, for the field was reduced to its present thirty-three starters the following year. That year, 1934, Mauri started fourth in a Leon Duray car and finished second with it. The car was fast, though not the fastest in the field. It handled badly and gave Rose a rough ride. It was such a rough ride that Duray called Shaw into the pits to relieve Rose, but Mauri refused to be relieved and carried on. He moved up as the leaders fell out, but finished twenty-seven seconds after Wild Bill Cummings in one of the dominant Millers.

For the next five races Rose's cars qualified four to six miles slower than the fastest cars in the competition. It was the car, not the driver, because when Rose got a car that was fast, in 1941, he put it on the pole. Before that his cars simply had little speed. He qualified them as far up front as he could and raced them as hard as he could. In 1935, his car came apart just past the halfway point and he placed twentieth. In 1936, he went all the way and he drove a steady race to finish fourth, only a few seconds short of third. He went on to score so consistently on the title trail that he won the driving crown. In 1937, at Indy, he was close to contention at 330 miles when his oil line snapped.

Rose's opportunities improved shortly before the war. In 1938, when Shaw ordered a Maserati to go with what he called his "pay car," he signed Rose to pilot one of the machines. When Wilbur decided the Maserati was underpowered, Mauri had to take that car while Shaw went into the old car. Mauri did a marvelous job in the slow car, skillfully guiding it into fifth place before it expired from the strain less than 100 miles from the finish. The following year, Rose moved into Shaw's "pay car" while Wilbur took over the improved Maserati. Rose finished eighth in the four-year-old machine, while Wilbur won his second 500.

Shaw said, "He did a superb job. I thought he would have trouble even finishing tenth against the new cars in the field."

Rose said, "I got what the car had to give me. You have to know your cars to get out of them what they have. You can only push them so far, and you have to find out how far. Smart driving can move you up a place or two, past faster cars that are driven badly. You have to drive with your head as well as your foot. I never cared about having the fastest speeds. I cared first about finishing. You have to finish to finish first."

Wilbur Shaw's Maserati was so far superior to its foes that if it did not break, it could not be beaten. Certainly, Shaw would not be outdriven. Rose, Rex Mays, Ted Horn and Joe Thorne drove with him for half the race in 1940, but then Shaw took command and pulled away. Mays finished second, Rose third, Horn fourth and Thorne fifth.

Reluctant to continue settling for Shaw's leftovers, Rose left Wilbur's bunch to begin searching for competitive cars to drive in the big one. He came close in 1940. He hit the jackpot in 1941. He landed a ride in one of the two Lou Moore cars and won with the second one.

Former driver Moore's masterfully prepared machines were not as good as the Maserati, but better than anything else in the field. Rose put his on the pole at better than 128 miles per hour and, after it broke down at 150 miles, took over the other at 180 miles. He moved steadily up from twelfth place to finish first after Shaw's

Maserati was wrecked at 375 miles. The car handled so smoothly it required only one pit stop for fuel, and they did not change a tire the entire distance. Mauri outdueled Mays in the closing stages, while luckless Ted Horn, making a mighty move up from twenty-eighth starting position, settled for third place.

The Moore team picked up almost $30,000 from Rose's ride, Mauri pocketed the driver's usual 40 percent cut and was in a position to demand more, as well as a guaranteed contract, for each season after that, but the war intervened and the squeeze on rubber, metal and fuel finished off the 500 and the other races for the duration. Rose and Shaw were at their peaks and were hurt more than most other drivers of the day by the suspension of their profession. It is not a bad bet that but for the break Rose or Shaw might have wound up with a fourth Indianapolis triumph, which eluded so many great drivers in this race.

When racing resumed in 1946, Shaw had retired, but Rose persisted. Mauri never did drive as many races as most racers. In the postwar years he limited himself mainly to the big one. A gentleman racer, this reserved little mustachioed fellow with the pipe in his mouth at all times away from the track and that old-fashioned visorless helmet on his head at all times on the track was the first dominant driver after the war.

Rose's old Moore machine was not competitive in 1946 in the first race after the war. It qualified ten miles per hour slower than the fastest car. Trying to keep it competitive, Mauri drove it hard until his steering failed. He spun, hit a wall and was tossed out, unhurt. This scared him. Nor was Shaw's old Maserati any longer strong enough. Ted Horn handled it smoothly but was fortunate to finish third with it after spending a lot of time in the pits having engine work done. George Robson beat Jimmy Jackson to the checker as old car after old car expired and only seven cars finished.

Only a few new cars were ready for this first postwar race. One was an experimental twin-engine machine that Paul Russo put on the front row but rammed against a barrier and wrecked early in the race. Another was a superpowered creation of Lou Welch of Novi, Michigan, which expired at 305 miles.

The "Novi," as it was nicknamed and as it remained known even as it passed from hand to hand from year to year, began as a souped-up V-8 engine designed in 1941, housed in an ancient car. It was driven to a fourth-place finish that year by Ralph Hepburn. Placed in a streamlined front-drive chassis in 1946, it was not ready to qualify on the opening day of time trials, so forfeited its shot at the pole, claimed by Cliff Bergere at 126 miles per hour. However, Hepburn later put it in the field with a new record speed of almost 134 miles per hour.

Thus, it burst into prominence spectacularly and became the most popular, but one of the most disappointing entries of the postwar period.

For most of the first 50 laps of the 1946 race, the Novi stole the show. Hepburn charged it from nineteenth starting spot to first place within the first 50 laps and was pulling away when its brakes began to fail. A prolonged pit stop for repairs dropped him back to thirteenth place before he could resume the race. He continued his charge and was closing in on the lead again when the engine came apart.

Crowds roared for the Novi, but some of the greatest racing mechanics tried and failed to harness properly its super power and some of the greatest racing drivers failed with it in the years to come.

The new cars that stole the spotlight in 1947 were Lou Moore's front-drive Offy-powered Blue Crown Specials, piloted by the skillful veteran Mauri Rose and a brilliant rookie, Bill Holland. Rookies do not usually win this race, which requires experienced driving, but Bill Holland, a rookie, but no kid at the advanced age of thirty-nine, came close in what was to be the most controversial of these classic contests.

The old Maserati still was swift and Horn put it on the pole, but could get it home no higher than third for the second straight year as the Blue Crowns easily outran it over the route. Cliff Bergere qualified a Novi second fastest, but it failed fast in the race. Rose filled out the front row in one of the Moore machines, while Holland put the other in the third row, and the race came down to a duel between them.

A driver's strike led by Hepburn, demanding a greater share in the race earnings, was headed off by Shaw, but it put some top drivers on the sidelines and held the starting field to thirty cars, even with the last minute addition of four cars.

Holland fell far back when he slid off the track avoiding a fatal crash by Shorty Cantlon. But then Holland drove like a demon and pulled far in front. Only Rose could keep up with the leader, but he preferred to lay back rather than risk ruining his car by keeping such a prodigious pace. Holland's car held together, however, and at 400 miles led Rose by two miles. Holland had been lapping all the other cars and admitted later he thought he had lapped Rose, also.

Moore didn't care which of his cars won. Ideally, he wanted them to finish one-two. He said later his main thought was that they not be ruined by a race to the finish between them. As Holland and Rose had been flashing past the pits, Moore's crewmen had been holding up blackboards with "P1" and "P2" chalked on them to inform the drivers of their positions. Now, he had his men give them the message "EZ." Assuming he was safely in front, Holland slowed to an easy pace.

Knowing Holland was within reach, Rose wanted to win, however. This is not truly a team sport. It is an individual competition and team drivers keep only the purses they themselves earn. With 100 miles more to run, Mauri made his move. Increasing his speed, he pressed his car to its limits. He began to cut two to three seconds a lap off Holland's lead.

With 20 laps left, Rose was within 30 seconds. With 15 laps left, Rose was within a straightaway of Holland and had the other car in his sights. With seven laps left, Rose caught and passed Holland. Believing Mauri was a lap back and was merely unlapping himself and gunning for runnerup honors, Holland simply smiled and waved encouragement to his teammate as he saw the sister car slip by.

Holland had no reason to think otherwise. Moore was flashing him the "OK" sign on every turn past the pits now. The next time around, the Moore pits displayed the "P1" sign to Rose, but replaced it with another "OK" sign for Holland. The cars continued at their pace toward the finish. Rose received the checkered flag at the conclusion of the 200th lap, 28 seconds ahead of Holland. Rose drove into Victory Lane. Holland couldn't believe what he was seeing and was furious.

Holland demanded an explanation from Moore. Moore merely said he didn't want a duel to the death between his own cars. Holland stormed away angrily, saying, "I don't know if he was playing favorites or what, but if you can't depend on your own crew to tell you the score, who can you count on? I could have won this race easily. I deserved to win. It's too big a race to be cheated out of it."

At the annual victory dinner, toastmaster Tommy Milton, the first two-time winner of this event, said in introducing Holland, "It is up to the driver of a car to know what he is doing in a race. I'm sure Holland realizes that now." Holland held his anger and admitted he realized that all too well now. And he accepted the second-place check of $31,300, which came close to Rose's $35,125 payoff because of almost $15,000 in bonuses for laps Holland led.

In introducing the new two-time Indy victor, Rose, Milton playfully suggested Mauri might admit who really had driven the best race. The sly Rose smiled and surprised everyone by saying, "I guess we all know who really drove the best race—Ted Horn." At that point the crowd came to its feet for a standing ovation, not for Rose, nor Holland, but for Horn, who had lost his hopes in the pits and as usual been beaten by this frustrating track.

The following year, Horn finished fourth in the 500 to give him four fourth-place finishes, four third-place finishes and a second-place finish in nine straight Indianapolis events, without having won one. And late in the year, after having clinched his third consecutive national driving title, the immortal Ted Horn was killed in a crash on the dirt at DuQuoin, Illinois.

That year, 1948, Mauri Rose took the checkered flag at Indy for the second straight year to become the third three-time winner of the great event. Holland had debated departing the Moore team, but decided to remain for the reason that the Moore cars were the best in competition. However, Holland's hopes for revenge on Rose went awry as Mauri simply outran Bill in their companion cars.

In practice before the race, Ralph Hepburn had been killed in a Novi. In the race itself, Horn's Maserati and Rex Mays's car swapped the lead back and forth for 200 miles before Duke Nalon's Novi shot to the front at the midway mark. Rose took over the top spot at 300 miles after the Novi lost time in the pits. Mays's car cracked. Holland passed Horn. When the Novi ran into fuel problems, Holland passed Nalon. But Holland could not keep up with Rose. Holland finished almost two minutes back as Rose roared across the finish line first for the third time.

Disputes over whether he deserved full credit for his triple crown notwithstanding, Rose coasted into Victory Lane, smiled as his crew swarmed all over him in happiness, and calmly commented, "It's an honor to have joined such select company." The payoff to the team was more than $60,000, with $42,800 of it coming from Rose's first-place finish. No other team has ever placed one-two in two consecutive years at Indy.

The Moore team made it three victories in a row in 1948, but this time it was Holland, not Rose, who took the triumph.

It was a year in which three-time winner Shaw called on two-time winner Milton to help him operate the Speedway. Pressured by driver demands to share the wealth that increasingly enormous crowds at this classic contest were creating, prize money had climbed above $100,000 for the first time in 1947, and would top $200,000 within five years. Reluctantly, Milton accepted the non-paying post of chief steward and commenced a four-year span of supervising the race that had brought him his greatest glory.

The Novis had been developed to their peak by 1949. Nalon and Mays had been hired to pilot sister cars. Nalon put his on the pole at almost 133 miles per hour, while Mays placed second fastest in the time trials. And when the green flag flew, Nalon and Mays ran far in front of the field. But on the twenty-third lap, leader Nalon was thrown into the wall when the rear axle on his Novi snapped and the left rear wheel broke off and bounded away. The car spun and backed along the barrier aflame for 200 feet as the fuel tank ruptured and exploded. It was the most spectacular single-car accident in the history of the track. Films of it frequently appear in racing movies and when you watch them it is difficult to believe Nalon suffered no serious injuries. Within 60 miles, Mays, too, was out of it in the other Novi, his massive powerplant stalled. This was the two-time national champion's twelfth and last try to win the elusive Speedway crown. In November, he was thrown from his car and killed in an accident in a car race on the horse-racing track at Del Mar, California.

When the Novis fell out, Lee Wallard fell into the lead, but he too fell out, with a fuel-tank failure, at 130 miles. Suddenly, Holland and Rose, in their now-aging but still-able Blue Crown racers, were running up front, and right behind them another Moore racer, a new one chauffeured by George Connor. On this Memorial Day, however, it was Holland's day at last. His pit crew played fair with him, but he took no chances. His car was running better than Rose's and he drove it harder, pulling more than a minute in front. When Rose's engine gave way and his car stalled 20 miles from the finish, Holland was home free and eased off.

Rookie Johnnie Parsons passed Connor in the last laps to prevent another one-two finish for the Moore forces, but Holland finished

24 seconds in front. The first-place prize topped $50,000 for the first time.

As Shaw had before him, Rose had hoped for a third straight 500 victory in vain. However, he still had hopes of a fourth 500 victory. Meanwhile, Holland had hopes of joining the select few who had won two in a row. And Holland had a proven car going for him, while Rose did not.

The performance of Parsons in a rear-drive machine in the late stages of the 1949 event impressed Rose to the point where he wanted a similar creation from Moore for 1950. Moore refused, so Rose went into another sponsor's front-drive car, while Holland remained with his old Moore machine.

Change occurs suddenly at Indy. Master mechanics maneuver for advantage. A dominant creation is imitated, then improved. Someone comes up with something different and better and the trend turns in a twinkling.

Copying the Parsons car, Frank Kurtis came up with a smaller, lighter machine than its rivals for sponsor J. C. Agajanian. A small, but brave rookie, Walt Faulkner, shocked the Speedway crowd by driving it to new time-trial records of 136 miles per hour for one lap and 134 for four in the final seconds of the first qualifying day, shattering the marks of the massive Novi. Then, when Faulkner faded in the race itself, Parsons' car darted nimbly around the course to lead by 38 seconds when a rainstorm aborted the 1950 event at 345 miles. Thus, a new day had dawned with the small light, rear-drive cars in command.

Holland's Blue Crown car could not keep up with Parsons' modern machine, nor could Rose's new mount. At the finish, Holland was 38 seconds back, Rose 1 minute and 49 seconds behind. And the domination of Blue Crown, of Rose and of Holland, had ended.

After having won the 500 once and finished second three times in one of the finest five-year runs the Speedway has seen, the maverick Holland denied himself a good chance to win this one more than once when he broke with Blue Crown, Moore and the AAA, and began to barnstorm on the "outlaw" tracks. Suspended by the sanctioning body for a while, he appeared only once more at Indy, in 1953, finishing far back in fifteenth place, and concluded his curious career in obscurity.

Meanwhile, Mauri Rose made one last try for his fourth win at Indianapolis in 1951, but his car was not competitive. A wheel broke and his mount overturned at 315 miles, but he escaped uninjured. He announced his retirement even as Lee Wallard was accepting the winner's laurels in Victory Lane.

Rose was a master of this track. Others drove it harder. Others were more daring. Many more led it many more laps. But in his fifteen consecutive starts, a record until recent times, Rose learned how to get the most out of his cars without breaking them. He drove 6,050 miles at the Speedway. Only Cliff Bergere ever endured more miles there, and Bergere never got from cars what Rose did, never winning with them as Rose did with his.

In retirement, Rose became an engineering specialist with various automotive and racing firms and a sort of elder statesman of the 500. Many years after he retired, Rose was impressed by a rookie and went to his sponsor and offered to teach him the tricks of the track.

He told J. C. Agajanian, "I've been watching your boy, and I think for his first year he's fantastic, and I'd like to talk to him because I think I can help him. I'm not doing anything around here, and I don't mean anything to anybody anymore, but I know this racetrack, and I know this race, and I think I can take some of what I've learned out of my head and put it in his head."

It was sad, this long-neglected immortal, hanging around at the arena where he first found fame, having to ask to help a hopeful. Agajanian, a compassionate person, agreed. He knew the cars were different than those Rose drove, and speeds at the Speedway far greater, but he also knew Mauri Rose had known the shortest way around once.

"You don't want to confuse a kid, but I felt the advice of a man like Mauri had to help more than it could hurt," Aggie recalls.

He took Rose to Parnelli Jones and it is a tribute to Parnelli that he recognized what Rose had done in the past and was eager to get from him what he had to give. Rose tutored Jones intensively and Parnelli went on to his own success. "I might have made it without Mauri, but you never know," Parnelli admitted later. "I got to the Speedway and I got fast in a hurry and impressed hell out of everyone, including me, but then I found I couldn't go any faster, and I had to go faster to make it. Not many noticed, but Mauri did. This is a very tricky track and Rose taught me some things that turned the trick for me. He got me to thinking about things so I could start to figure them out for myself."

Rose has explained, "Indianapolis is a much flatter track than more modern ovals. It doesn't have Daytona's banking, for example. It's much more demanding than Daytona. You can't maintain speed all the way around here as you can at Daytona. You have to drive your way around the Indianapolis track. You have to accelerate and brake, slow down and speed up. Every turn is different. You have to find how deep you can drive into every corner. You have to know when to get on and off the accelerator.

"The harder you try here, the slower you go sometimes. Smoothness matters more than anything else. You have to find the fastest groove all the way around. It may be high in one place, low in another. You get a groove going for you. It was true in my day, it's true today. It was just as hard to drive right in my day as it is today. The cars are faster today, but better. The track has been completely paved and is smoother. You never could afford to make many mistakes."

Rose sighed, "No one thought the lessons I learned in my day could be applied to today, but if I helped one new driver I'm happy. The problem with being the best driver you can be is that by the time you've found out what you need to know and got it into your head, you've lost what you need physically from your body. It's a sport that needs old heads and young bodies. But it's a sport of speed and no matter how smart you get, when you slow down you've got to get out."

Rose knew it was time for him the day he retired in 1951. It had been nineteen years since Mauri had moved onto the Indianapolis oval for the first time. He had hoped to run one more year to make it twenty, but he had run out of time. Two bad accidents in the past five races convinced him it was time to quit.

"I'm not as sharp as I was," he said. "I'm running too great a risk to keep racing. I'm an old man in a young man's game. I'll leave it to the kids," a contented Rose sighed as he sat grease-smeared, sore and weary in his garage later, puffing on his pipe, presuming his prominence would endure forever.

There *were* "kids" coming along, too, including one daring young man, Bill Vukovich, who went unnoticed when he finished far back in twenty-ninth place as a rookie in Rose's last race, but the following year would begin a brilliant, but bitterly brief run at immortality. This would bring him into the select circle of two-time winners and almost put him out of reach as the winner of four in a row before the fates felled him.

The run of one Indianapolis immortal ends and the run of another begins. It almost always has been this way at "The Brick-yards."

5 *Bill Vukovich*

1953, 1954

"You put your foot all the way into it and keep turning left. It's just that damn simple," Bill Vukovich once said. It is not that simple. It was not for him. But that was the way he looked at it. You either did it or you didn't, this deadly dangerous thing he did. You either went all the way with it, or you walked away from it.

Bill Vukovich did not walk away from it. He went all the way with it, and was carried away in the end. It killed him, this hard, cold, arrogant, almost mean man, but he seemed driven by some dream of destiny to pursue his passion until it caught up with him, one of the greatest Indianapolis drivers ever, on the verge of the greatest record ever put together at the Speedway.

Through the 1975 race at Indy, 19 men have been killed practicing or qualifying for the race, 18 men have died in the race itself. Of the 36 men who have won the 58 classics, 13 have been killed in other races, but 23 have so far survived their sport, and most have retired before it could claim them.

Only two Indianapolis winners have been killed at Indianapolis, only one of whom won this great race more than once. Oddly, death claimed each the year after his 500 victory. Floyd Roberts, who beat Wilbur Shaw in 1938, returned in 1939 to cartwheel over a wall into a fence and be thrown to his death. And Bill Vukovich, who won two straight 500's in 1953 and 1954, was leading in 1955 when death claimed him at the tail end of a multicar crackup. There was nothing he could do. It was done to him.

"I don't think about death," he once said. "We all die. I was born, I'll die. One way or another. Racing or not racing. I don't know if race drivers rush it. I don't want to know," he said, and walked away, going his own way, as he always did.

Bill Vukovich was born in 1919 in Alameda, California, one of eight children. Two years later, the family moved to a farm outside of Fresno. Here, Bill was reared, in the fields, working hard. School did not interest him much. Sports did to some extent, but he was not a big boy, he did not have great all-around athletic ability, and he was not a joiner who liked team games.

When he was thirteen, his father died. Bill and his two brothers picked cotton and vegetables in the fields, drove trucks and pruned trees to help their mother make ends meet. She died when Bill was sixteen. He lived with older relatives, but the family began to come apart. He dealt with death early in life and he grew up without much, leading a hard life. He wanted a way out, to a better life.

"You find what you can do and you do it," he said.

He was eighteen when he persuaded a friend to let him drive in a stock-car race in 1937. He liked cars and speed and felt no fear. "If you're afraid to live, you might as well be dead," he once said. He was not afraid and he began to race cars for a living. It was not much of a living at first and he worked in garages on the side to keep going. He did not eat a lot and did not care about fancy clothes. He did not go out a lot. His life was the race track. He was a loner.

He was only nineteen when he crashed in his first midget-car race and cracked his collarbone and three ribs. But after he recovered, he resumed his career. He crashed often, but recovered and kept on racing. He was too tough at this time, too impatient to succeed. He wasn't smart enough about racing to realize you can't push a car as far as you can push yourself.

Some weeks he raced as many as fifteen to twenty times in small events on bad tracks. There were weeks in which he won some races and wound up with $40 to $60 dollars profit and weeks in which he did not win any races and wound up with nothing. He'd had a hard time all his life and racing didn't change that for a number of years. For a while a brother, Eli, also drove the tour in central and northern California, but he gave up eventually. Bill did not give up.

When World War II broke out and racing ended for the duration, Bill sat it out, working in a repair shop. He had found a woman who cared for him and could accept his moody ways and with whom he could have companionship. He married her. A son was born, Bill, Jr., in 1944. Vukovich was no longer alone in life, though beyond his home he was as much a loner as ever.

When peace returned, Vukovich returned to his personal war. By then he had matured. He was in his late twenties. Time was running out on him and his hope of making his way to the top in racing. He was ready to make the most of his daring and ability, and determined to do so.

He was a hard man to get to know well and hard to like. Car owners did not dare tell him what to do with their cars, although they ran the financial risks with them. "I risk my neck. I decide what I do when I drive," he said. But his skill began to get him good rides. He began to win, began to get better rides and began to win more.

He won the West Coast midget-car driving championships in 1946 and 1947, took his car across country to challenge the best drivers in other areas, and captured the national crown in 1950. The postwar craze for midget cars peaked about this time, and attention turned to bigger cars—the sprinters and the championship cars. Vukie was ready to make his move to the title trail by then, anyway.

Small and gaunt, but strong and tough, he could manhandle a machine with the best of them. An almost humorless man, he drove with deadly determination.

Once, he drove in the 2,000-mile Pan American Road Race with Vern Houle, a fine mechanic, sitting alongside him as his navigator. Vukie drove so recklessly around the blind curves of the mountainous course that Houle was terrified and kept asking the racer to take it easy. For a long time, Vukie did not say anything. Then he missed a curve and the car went sailing off the side of a thirty-foot enbankment. The moment the car was airborne, Vukie took his hands off the steering wheel and said to Houle, "All right, you drive."

The car crashed. Somehow, both escaped critical injuries. But Houle never rode with Vukie again.

In 1950, Vukie invaded Indy. Fortunately, one-man cars had been established at Indianapolis in 1938, and he drove as he preferred to race—alone. In 1950 he did not have a good car, and his prominence in midget cars meant nothing. He passed his driver's test easily enough in an old, tired car, but he could not get it up to competitive speed and failed to qualify it to race. When someone sympathized with him, Vukie snapped, "I'll be back," and went on his way.

Nor was his car really competitive in 1951. He did get into the field for the first time, but way back in twentieth starting position. Before the race, he gloomily guessed, "This old crate will fall apart within thirty laps." He charged up to the top ten in the early stages of the event, but the car went out with a cracked oil tank at twenty-nine laps. "I'll be back with a better car," he vowed.

He was. His brief burst of showy driving had caught the eye of Howard Keck, a wealthy sponsor who had backed the building of a new balanced car created by Frank Kurtis. He called Vukie in Fresno and offered him the ride. The driver grabbed it because Kurtis was one of the most respected of the roadster-builders and seemed sure to have turned out a good piece of equipment.

The Kurtis car was not ready on the opening day of time trials, and Vukovich stormed around angrily as little Freddie Agabashian put a huge, experimental Don Cummins car with a diesel truck engine on the pole. He had a fast lap of 139.1 miles per hour and a four-lap average of 138.0 miles per hour, both records.

On the second day, Vukie startled the crowd with a Sunday drive at an average 138.2 miles per hour, including one lap at 139.4 to raise the records. Swiftly, he parked the car, climbed out of the cockpit and slipped away, eluding the crowd that was closing in.

While his crew was celebrating, Bill Vukovich sat alone in his garage, perched on the edge of a workbench, thinking his private thoughts. When reporters, searching for him, found him there, he was asked why he hadn't taken part in the triumphal proceedings. "Why in the hell should I?" he asked. "All those guys want to do is pound me on the back, or shake my hand, or ask me for an autograph. To hell with them."

Suddenly, he was a celebrity, and he hated it. He fled from his fame. He fled from his fans. He hated to sign autographs. He hated to make small-talk. He hated to talk at all. Cornered by a reporter, he would say straight out what he thought. He didn't care what others thought of it. Then he would walk away. He refused most formal requests for interviews. He shied from cameras. He slipped through the shadows while the spotlight sought him.

He hated being a hero. "The same people who cheer you when you win, boo you when you lose," he once said. "The people who write how great you are when you win make you look like a bum when you lose. The people who want to be your friend when you're on top forget you fast when you hit the skids. A man can't afford to have many friends. I don't have many, not even among drivers. I'm trying to beat them, not be buddies with them. We're all alone in this life. We do what we do on our own."

He was, whatever else he was, an honest man. He lived his life as he thought it should be lived. He gave no favors to anyone, and asked none, either. He was more admirable in his way than many who wear masks and pretend to be better than they are. Vukie had no pretense. He was a professional race driver. He raced to win. He raced for money, but he wanted to win more than he wanted the money. He took pride in his performances. He didn't care what others thought of them or of him. He set high standards for himself, but he cared only about satisfying himself.

He didn't say a single word when on the second and final weekend of qualifying Chet Miller in a Novi surpassed his records with speeds of 139.6 for one lap and 139.0 for four. Vukie believed he had the best car and he confided to his crew that he didn't expect the Novi or Diesel entries to endure the grueling race. They did not. The Novi went out at 41 laps and the Diesel at 71 laps, both with engine failures. Even earlier, a highly touted Ferrari driven by Grand Prix great Alberto Ascari had spun out after a wheel broke.

Having started eighth as a second-day qualifier, Vukovich charged his little car up through the pack from the instant the green flag unfurled. He was sixth after one lap and fourth after two. One more lap and he was third. After another lap, he was second. Within 20 miles, Vukie had moved past Jack McGrath to take the lead. Troy Ruttman, piloting a car sponsored by J. C. Agajanian, had followed him through the pack and kept on his tail.

Vukie pulled away from Ruttman, but when Bill made his two stops for fuel and tires, Ruttman took first place and pocketed lap-leading money for a while before he, too, had to pit and relinquish the lead. After his last stop, however, Vukie began to pull far in front, lap after lap.

His car was capable and he had become such a smooth chauffeur that he got it into its groove and ran it as though on rails, without any sign of trouble, passing and lapping slower cars without hesitation. Those who know a good driver when they see one in action were awed by the performance of this great driver who so suddenly had come into prominence.

Agajanian, the owner of Ruttman's car, later admitted, "I wanted my machine to win, but there was no way Ruttman could catch Vukovich unless something went wrong. None of us who were there will ever forget what a super performance that Californian put on. He was a natural. He drove the car hard, but he didn't make a mistake. He was bound to be great. If the car didn't break, he couldn't be beat."

The car began to break with 100 miles left when he was almost two miles in the lead. He did not know it, but a pivot pin had cracked in his steering assembly. What he did know was that his steering had become difficult. He had to wrestle with the wheel just to keep the car on course. It was dangerous. Many others would have quit, but he did not.

He could not keep up his speed. Seeing the leader had slowed some, the Agajanian pit crew signaled Ruttman to push his car to the limits. Encouraged, Ruttman started to close in on Vukovich. With only ten laps left, Ruttman had moved within half a mile of Vukovich. But Bill still led, working hard in his cockpit to keep his car on course and hold his lead.

On the 191st lap, a little more than 20 miles from the finish, the pin broke apart, the steering went out completely, the car went out of control. Vukovich scraped it to a stop alongside a wall and climbed out of the crippled machine, cursing. He climbed atop the wall and sat there sullenly as Ruttman rode on to the coveted triumph and a $60,000 payoff.

Sixteen cars in all exceeded Vukie's laps before the event was flagged to a finish. He is listed as having finished seventeenth which shows how misleading such statistics are. He had been beaten and he was bitter.

He defied the fates. He said later, "It was lousy luck, that's all. I was beaten by my car, not the other car. This track isn't so tough. It's a cinch. I'll show you next year. I'll blow everyone off. All those hot dogs. All you have to do is drive faster than the other guy. You put your foot all the way into it and keep turning left. It's just that simple. There's nothing tough about it at all."

He showed them. He returned the next year, 1953, with a new

Keck car, punished it in practice and saw to it that it was ready by the opening day of qualification runs.

The weather wasn't right. Vukie went out for his ten-mile time trial with black stormclouds hovering overhead. He moved like a madman around that flat, 2½-mile oval. He was breaking all records when it began to rain on his fourth and final lap. He would not quit even as the track under his tires started to grow dangerously slick. He drove daringly as he shot over the slick surface of the straightaway. After that, he came to be called "The Mad Russian."

Only the rain refused him his records. Without traction, his last-lap speed had lessened and he had settled for a four-lap average above 138 miles per hour to capture the pole position. Soaked as he parked in a downpour, he allowed himself a rare smile as his crew, the officials and the reporters crowded in on him. He said a few words, thanking his crew for their help, and then he got away from there to his own world.

Indianapolis was an inferno on race day. The arena was a hell. Cars run hot anyway. Cramped in the cockpit, the drivers swelter. On a day like Memorial Day, 1953, the cars become ovens and the drivers within them are roasting.

By this time, few drivers were relieved in the races. For this race, most were. One after another, drivers pulled into the pits, requesting relief. The number of available relief drivers ran out. Some drivers simply stopped, pleading problems with their cars. They collapsed in their pits, sweating heavily.

On his pit stops, Vukovich simply spilled paper cups of cold water on his neck and down his back, and roared off. He drove like a demon. At the halfway point, he was four miles in front of the next nearest car.

As the race wore on under the blazing sun, fans fainted in the stands and the first-aid stations filled up. One by one, more cars dropped out of the chase. During the day, six cars smashed into walls, their drivers dazed and weakened by the smothering heat.

Vukovich drove on, pulling farther and farther in front, lap after lap. Asked in his pit if he wanted relief, he laughed and drove off. His car should have overheated, but it did not. It held together. He pushed it harder and harder. At the finish, he was eight miles in front.

Only five drivers were still running at the finish who had not required relief, and none of the others had run nearly as hard as Vukie. One of them, Carl Scarborough, was 35 miles back when he was flagged off the track. He crawled from the cockpit of his car and collapsed. He was hurried to the hospital, but he died of heat exhaustion.

After that, Vukovich came to be called "The Indianapolis Iron Man."

He accepted congratulations in Victory Lane with only occasional smiles and escaped the crowd as swiftly as he could. He collected a record share of nearly $90,000 from a record purse of nearly a quarter-of-a-million dollars.

Now, for the first time in his life, he no longer needed money. Now he no longer drove the entire tour. He couldn't have cared less about the national driving title or any other laurels. "I know who's the best," he grumbled. "No one else has to tell me. I'll be back for the big one."

He returned in 1954 to defend his Speedway crown. He had spent much of his time between races working out, running, squeezing a rubber ball in his powerful fingers, making his thin body muscular. He was a proud man, intense about the conditioning that kept him performing properly while rivals were wilting. He was in his mid-thirties, but he was not old. However, his car was old. He didn't want another car. He didn't want a new one. This one had won for him.

The car was coming apart all through the month of May. It seemed as if every time Vukie took it out to practice, something went wrong with it. The crew worked hard on it, but it was not ready to qualify on the first weekend of time trials. Vukie sulked as his anger grew. The crew continued to work hard. They had it ready by the final qualifying day, but by then six rows were filled in front of him.

Vukie qualified in the 138-mile-per-hour bracket, almost 3 mph slower than the pole-winner, Jack McGrath. Bill settled for nine-teenth starting spot, on the inside of the seventh row. Yet he remained confident that once in, he could win again.

Passing a group of drivers talking prior to the prerace meeting, Vukie laughed. "What are you guys up to?" he asked. "Trying to figure out who's going to finish second tomorrow?"

One of the drivers suggested Vukie, himself, starting so far back, would be fortunate to finish second. "If they offered me second-place money right now, I'd refuse," Vukovich said, scowling.

The day of the race Vukie carried in his pocket a note from his son, Bill, Jr. It read, "Dear Daddy, Smoke those hot dogs off the track." He would do just that.

"Gentlemen, start your engines!"

The scowling Californian hunched over the wheel and waited while they fired up his engine. The cars moved away, pulling into position, circling the track on their warmup laps. The fans came to their feet in anticipation. The green flag unfurled. The cars charged into the first turn in a streaming tangle of tight traffic, the thundering roar of engines and strong smell from their fuel fumes filling the air.

McGrath laid on a murderous pace out front, with Jimmy Bryan, Troy Ruttman, Johnny Thomson and Sam Hanks hanging on to him. Back in the pack, Vukovich began to pick off the cars in front of him, passing high, low, snaking his way through the field.

In the first 10 laps, he passed 10 cars. It began to get tougher, then, as the fast cars were left in front of him. At 50 miles, he was sixth. At 100 miles, fourth. At 150 miles, second. The Indianapolis Iron Man was cutting them down, one at a time. Now only McGrath, maintaining a record pace, was ahead of him. But Vukovich was maintaining a faster pace. Within a few laps he had caught up to and passed McGrath to take the lead as the crowd hollered for Vukie.

The pace was punishing for tires, and the drivers were making a record number of pit stops to replace rubber. McGrath had made one. Now Vukovich made one. And four cars, led by Mc-Grath, passed him before he returned to the race. It took him 30 laps to get the lead back, but he got it back. At 300 miles, he had moved in front of Bryan, McGrath and Art Cross, and a lap or more in front of the rest.

At 350 miles, Vukie pitted again, surrendering the lead again. At 375 miles, he regained the lead. He had no more pit stops scheduled now. The burly Bryan, who would win his first of three national titles that year, could not keep up. The luckless McGrath could not keep up. Young Ruttman could not keep up. A couple of cars had crashed. Now Pat O'Connor spun out. Then Jim Rathmann, relieving Sam Hanks, spun out. One of Vukie's tires began to wear dangerously thin. His pit crew called him in. He ignored the signals and kept going.

At the finish he was more than a lap in front of Bryan, McGrath, Ruttman and the rest. He swung into Victory Lane on a bad tire that was about to blow. His wife and crew and the crowd of officials and reporters surrounded him. He was handed an "extra" of the *Indianapolis News*, its headline printed trackside only minutes before. The headline read, "Vuky Wins Again." A rare grin creased his grease-stained face.

He got out of there into his garage, where he sat on a workbench, his wife by his side. His t-shirt was soiled and sweaty. His hands and arms were dirty and sore. His face suddenly seemed old, creased with weariness. The Indianapolis Iron Man was worn out.

A photographer poked inside and snapped a picture, his flashbulb popping brightly in Vukie's face, making him frown. A reporter pressed up to him and asked him how he felt. Vukovich cocked his head. He could not hear. The roar of the engines had deadened his hearing for the time being. The question was repeated, more loudly. Vukie heard. "How do you think I feel?" he asked.

The purse surpassed a quarter-million dollars for the first time. It hit almost $270,000. Vukie's team collected almost $90,000. Vukie pocketed his share, his wife packed, and they went away. "I'll be back," he said again.

He was the third driver, following Wilbur Shaw and Mauri Rose, to win two in a row. It easily could have been three in a row. Now he wanted to make it three in a row in 1955. If he could, he would be the first driver ever to do that. "I want to do what no one else has ever done," he said, back home.

"It won't be easy," someone said.

"It never is," he said, and turned away.

It was a fateful 500 in 1955. Two-time winner Tommy Milton had retired as chief steward. Three-time winner Wilbur Shaw had been buried, killed in a plane crash the preceding fall. Manuel Ayulo was killed in a practice crash prior to the race.

Seeking to become a three-time winner, Bill Vukovich had lost his sponsor. Howard Keck felt he had gotten all he could out of racing and had gone back to business. Lindsey Hopkins, an Atlanta man made wealthy with Coca-Cola interests, had kept the winning team together and provided it with a new car that was a carbon copy of the old one.

Jack McGrath again topped the time trials with a speed of 142 miles per hour, but Bill Vukovich came close and qualified fifth fastest for a satisfactory starting spot in the middle of the second row. Still, he seemed to those who had come to know him to be growing uneasy as race day came near. He had even less to say than usual. He was not wisecracking with the other drivers. He was not taunting his rivals. He wanted to win, but he did not really like racing. The brighter the spotlight, the less he liked it.

The night before the race, on the eve of his bid for immortality, he said to his wife, "Esther, this is crazy. Let's go home." But they did not. On race morning, he stood near another driver, looked at

the fans, and said, "They think we're freaks. And you know something—they're right." And he climbed into the cockpit of his car
and waited, and when the green flag unfurled he drove with his
usual cold fury.

From the front row, McGrath sped into the first corner in front.
He held his lead for two full laps before Vukovich passed him.
McGrath hung hard on Vukie's tail, pressing him at suicidal speeds
as they pulled far in front of the pack. McGrath darted around
Vukovich on the fifteenth lap. Vukovich drove around McGrath
on the sixteenth lap. Still, McGrath stuck to his tailpipe. And on
the twenty-fifth lap, McGrath moved back in front. But a lap later,
Vukovich reclaimed the lead, driving the fastest lap ever recorded
in traffic to that time—more than 141 miles per hour.

It was a dramatic duel that kept the fans standing and screaming
from the start. Now, however, McGrath weakened. Passed three
times in thirty minutes, he could no longer keep up with the
punishing pace Vukovich was setting. Vukovich began to widen
the gap. After 50 laps, he was 15 seconds in front. A few laps later,
at 135 miles, the overworked engine in McGrath's car gave out
and he coasted into the pits, beaten again. Now there was no one
left to threaten Vukovich. If nothing went wrong. But something
went wrong.

Bill Vukovich in his Hopkins car was a half-mile in front of
Jimmy Bryan and Bob Sweikert as he sped along the backstretch
on his fifty-sixth lap, preparing to lap three tailenders who loomed
up in front of him. At that instant, an axle on Rodger Ward's car
snapped, the car lurched out of control, and overturned. Al Keller
cut his car to the left to avoid Ward's car, found himself headed
for a concrete support for a footbridge just off the racing surface,
swerved to his right, and sideswiped Johnny Boyd's car, knocking
it directly into the path of Vukovich's car.

The left front wheel of Vukie's car rode over the right rear wheel
of Boyd's car, snapping it off. Vukie's car rose, airborne, sailed over
the outer wall, rolled over in the air, hit the ground nose first,

bounced high in the air, turned end over end, spinning wildly, and came to a crashing rest upside down, exploding in flames. Bill Vukovich was already dead within, from a fractured skull.

The metal in cars can crack. The iron in men can be broken, too.

It was almost a half-hour before the track could be cleared so the remaining cars could resume racing speed. Jimmy Bryan inherited the lead, but his was the next car to fail. Bob Sweikert came into the lead and held it, with Tony Bettenhausen finishing second.

After Vukovich's death the AAA (American Automobile Association) decided to drop its sponsorship of car racing. USAC (the United States Auto Club) was formed to sanction the championship and associated circuits. Sweikert captured the national driving crown in 1955. But thirteen months after his Indianapolis success, he was killed in a racing accident at Salem, Indiana.

Jimmy Bryan won the next two national titles. Then Tony Bettenhausen captured his second crown. Pat Flaherty and Sam Hanks won Indy in 1956 and 1957 respectively. Bryan won Indianapolis in 1958. He retired for a while, then resumed racing. He was killed in a racing accident at Langhorne, Pennsylvania, in 1960. Bettenhausen was killed in a practice crash at Indianapolis the following year as he was preparing for his fifteenth 500. He had the fast car that year and was favored, but he was fatally injured testing a friend's car.

Bettenhausen never won at Indianapolis. His sons have wanted to win for him, but it has eluded them. Gary almost won once and is still trying, but since has suffered a serious injury at Syracuse, leaving one arm limp. Another son, Merle, lost an arm in a racing accident, raced on a while, then retired. Tony, Jr., tried it in stock cars, but without success.

Bill Vukovich, Jr., has also become a race driver. He once said, "I didn't really want it, but the world seemed to want it for me. I don't like it all that much, but I do it. It is like it is my life and was bound to be." He is much as his father was—withdrawn, tough, difficult to talk to or get to know. As his father was, he is a very private person who prefers slipping through shadows to being in the spotlight.

Bill, Jr., is good and could win Indianapolis some May. He was Rookie of the Year there in 1968. He was the first driver to break through the barriers of both 180 and 185 miles per hour there in a blazing qualifying run in 1972. He placed second there in 1973 and third in 1974. He has also placed third at Ontario, California, and fourth and fifth at Pocono, Pennsylvania, in 500-mile races on the two Indianapolis-style tracks that opened in the 1970's.

He has a son, Bill Vukovich, III. Bill, Jr., says, "My dad wanted me to be a race driver, but I don't want my son to have anything to do with racing. It is dangerous. It killed my father before my son was born. All my father thought about was racing, racing, racing. I think about other things. I want my son to think about other things. I want to play baseball with my son. My father didn't play baseball with me. My father was the type man that I was never with him. My father didn't do anything with us. I want my wife and I to do everything with our son."

Bill Vukovich, Sr., was killed in the first car Lindsey Hopkins sponsored at Indianapolis. Tony Bettenhausen was driving for Hopkins there the year he was killed. Hopkins has been sponsoring entries at Indianapolis all these years and has yet to win there. Bill Vukovich won there twice, but if all had gone well he could well have won four 500's in a row at that ominous oval.

The accident that claimed his life in his mid-thirties was set off by the collapse of the car driven by young Rodger Ward, who was to go on to become the next driver to win this difficult classic twice. He picked up the baton that had been dropped by the pacesetter, you might say. The chain remains unbroken. Runners drop out, but the race goes on.

Victory Lane, 1964; A. J. Foyt acknowledges cheers, wife by his side, after 500 win in which Eddie Sachs and Dave MacDonald died.

Left: Rodger Ward, 1959. Right: Parnelli Jones bails out of burning car in pits, 1964.

Rodger Ward in A. J. Watson's Leader Card Special roadster, which took him to his second triumph, in 1962.

Winner
Rodger Ward 1962 Indianapolis Motor Speedway

WINNER
A.J.FOYT·1961·INDIANAPOLIS MOTOR SPEEDWAY

A. J. Foyt in George Bignotti's Bowes Seal Fast Special roadster, which carried him to triumph in 1961.

Foyt in Shearton-Thompson Special, the new-styled rear-engine lightweight which carried him to his third victory, in 1967.

"WINNER"
A.J.FOYT·1967·INDIANAPOLIS MOTOR SPEEDWAY

A. J. Foyt leads Eddie Sachs in late stages of dramatic duel at Indy in 1961 that brought Foyt his first 500 victory and doomed the dream of Sachs.

A. J. Foyt chases eventual winner Rodger Ward in 1962.

Typical Indianapolis pit stop shows Rodger Ward getting help everywhere at once from the crew of A. J. Watson (center foreground) in 1964.

Beautifully-balanced Foyt car comes around a corner en-route to 1967 Indianapolis triumph.

Al Unser zips past blurred fans on his way to his first 500 victory in 1970.

Al Unser perched on Parnelli Jones's Johnny Lightning Special, the George Bignotti-prepared car which took him to his second straight triumph in 1971.

"WINNER"

AL UNSER INDIANAPOLIS MOTOR SPEEDWAY 197

Victory Lane, 1971: Al Unser smiles at boss, balding former 500 winner Parnelli Jones, after his second straight championship drive in Indianapolis 500.

Master mechanic George Bignotti, right, congratulates Al Unser after his 1971 victory. Bignotti was the man behind the man in the victories by Al in '70 and '71, A. J. Foyt in '61 and '64 and Gordon Johncock in '73, giving him a record five Indianapolis 500 triumphs as a mechanic. Bignotti also won the California 500 in 1971 with Joe Leonard and in 1973 with Roger McCluskey and the Pennsylvania 500 in 1972 with Leonard.

Bird's-eye view of winning Eagle of Bobby Unser, 1968.

Bobby Unser on way out of pits and back to track in '68 victory.

Foyt, 1968.

A. J. Foyt, 1974.

A. J. Foyt, 1974, with winged car.

Three-time winner A. J. Foyt preparing to step into his Indianapolis car in 1972.

Foyt, 1973.

Bobby Unser.

A jubilant Bobby Unser prepares to enter Victory Lane, 1968.

Bobby and Al Unser, 1970.

Al Unser, on the main straightaway, 1971.

Bobby Unser pulling away from his pit at completion of stop, 1975.

Bobby Unser on the main straightaway, 1975.

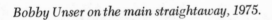

A rain-damp Bobby Unser acknowledges the cheers of the crowd in 1975 after becoming the seventh driver in history to win the Indianapolis 500 more than once.

6   *Rodger Ward*

1959, 1962

When he crashed at Indy in 1955, setting off the chain-reaction collision that claimed the life of Bill Vukovich, Rodger Ward was in the midst of a prolonged period of failure such as has frustrated many men for many years before they went on to attain the summit at Indianapolis eventually.

Ward was born in Beloit, Kansas, in January, 1921, but reared in southern California. As a boy he was attracted to exciting, dangerous activities. He says that all he can remember of his childhood is wanting to grow up to be an airplane pilot or a race-car driver. He learned to fly fighter planes during World War II, although he did not see any action. After the war, he began to race cars, mostly midgets, which were at the peak of their popularity at that time in the Los Angeles area.

Rodger had an ability to handle a car at speed from the start, but for a long time he was something less than serious about his sport, and for many years he was just another driver. A good-looking fellow with a lot of dark, curly hair and an engaging smile, he loved the ladies, liked to party, and swiftly spent whatever money he made at the tracks.

"All I cared about," he has admitted, "was having a good time."

With experience, however, he began to win. In 1951 he was offered a ride at Indianapolis and accepted it. It was not a very good ride. It was to be a long time before he got a good ride there. Sponsors were reluctant to back this playboy with good equipment. Still, he kept going back.

"I was having a good time," he has said. "I was an Indianapolis driver and that meant something, even if I wasn't a winner. It would have been almost impossible for me to win with the cars I had there at first. I just drove them as good as I could until they couldn't go any farther and then went out and had a good time."

In his first eight years in the 500, he qualified among the first ten cars only once and finished in the top ten only once. He qualified tenth in 1953 and finished eighth in 1956. Most of the time his time-trial speeds were way back in the field and he finished way back. Six of the eight years he didn't even finish in the top twenty.

After he finished thirtieth in 1957 and twentieth in 1968, no one thought much of him as a driver, and no one considered him among the ones who might win this classic contest. This is a mistake because Indianapolis history is replete with the records of veteran drivers who were failures here for many years before finally succeeding, often after getting good equipment for the first time.

Such was the case during Ward's days at Indy in the 1950's. Lee Wallard was an established driver when he won in 1951, Ward's rookie year, but Troy Ruttman, Bill Vukovich and Bob Sweikert seemed to come out of nowhere into Victory Lane in the years immediately following. Pat Flaherty hadn't come close to winning when he came home first ahead of Sam Hanks in 1956. Hanks hadn't come close for ten years before he came in second in 1956 and then first in 1957. Jimmy Bryan had won everywhere else, but a second one year and a third another year were the best he could do in six years at Indy before he won the event in 1958 after a first-lap crackup that wrecked eight cars and killed driver Pat O'Connor.

Hanks and Bryan won with the same car. Hanks retired after his 1957 victory and Bryan took his car to the 1958 victory. George Salih, chief mechanic of Lee Wallard's earlier victory, had constructed a streamlined roadster with the conventional Meyer-Drake Offie lying unconventionally on its side to increase the car's balance. It was in this car that skilled drivers such as Hanks and Bryan could finally come through at the Speedway.

However, another master mechanic, A. J. Watson, who had originally come to Indianapolis with a car built in his backyard, "The Pots and Pans Special," remained convinced that the way to go was to lighten the car without altering the upright position of the engine. He built one which Jim Rathmann drove to victory by a big margin over defending champion Jimmy Bryan in the second and last of two international 500's at Monza, Italy, in 1958.

For the 1959 Indianapolis race, Watson constructed two new upright cars, selling one to the Rathmann team and the other to the Rodger Ward team, backed by Bob Wilke of Milwaukee. Watson then joined the Wilke entry as chief mechanic of the Leader Card Special.

For the first time, Ward had quality around him, but the favorites remained defending champion Bryan in his two-time winner and Johnny Thomson in another horizontal creation. Thomson put his car on the pole at almost 146 miles per hour. Rathmann qualified third fastest, Ward sixth fastest.

Bryan, who had only recently emerged from a brief retirement, had lost his edge and never was a factor. He qualified far back and his weary car quit at the start of the race. However, the other three engaged in one of the most thrilling races Indianapolis has had, one that kept the fans in a frenzy through the long, hot afternoon.

All were hungry. Thomson, a small, tousle-haired fellow of thirty-seven, a demon on dirt, had been driving twenty years elsewhere with success, but six years on the smooth surface of the Speedway without success. Rathmann, a slender, balding, thirty-year-old veteran of a dozen years in racing, now raced rarely anywhere but Indianapolis, but had settled for second twice without winning. This was his tenth try. Ward, short and stocky at thirty-eight, had won seven times on the championship trail. He knew he could run with the others even if few experts did.

He said later, "When I slipped into the cockpit of that car, took it out on the track and began to drive it, a thrill shot over me. I could see this was a car that could win. It sobered me up. It made me think of all my wasted years. My competitive career was getting away from me. Already, I no longer was a kid. Time was running out. I figured it was now or never. I was serious about racing for the first time, really."

At the green flag, Thomson thrust his shocking-pink speedster into the first corner in front, with Ward's white, red and blue machine moving right behind him. At the 15-mile mark, Ward passed Thomson, Rathmann burst into third with his blue and orange racer, and the three started to pull away from the rest of the field. At 50 miles, Rathmann passed Thomson and Ward, and surged to the front.

Lap after lap, the three battled for the lead, while the huge crowd cheered them on and the other drivers struggled desperately to remain in contention. Eddie Sachs spun his car, but maintained control and continued on. Len Sutton walloped the southwest wall. Red Amick, Mike Magill, Jud Larson and Chuck Weyant locked into a four-car crackup that put them all out of the race. Jack Turner's car burst into flames and he fled from it.

Cars kept dropping out while the three leaders poured it on. They swept in and out of their pits, picking up fuel and tires in less than 30 seconds sometimes. At 150 miles, Thomson had taken the lead. Ward passed him. Then Thomson passed Ward. Then Rathmann passed Ward. The lead shifted spectacularly. At the halfway point Ward had moved back in front, with Thomson second and Rathmann third.

Round and round the cars rolled, engines whining, tires shrieking, metal bodies straining, the drivers hot and sweaty and tiring under the struggle. Ray Crawford's car crashed the northeast barrier. At 150 laps, with just 50 of the 2½-mile laps left, Ward remained ahead with the other two pursuing him relentlessly. At 400 miles Ward opened up about 400 yards on Thomson and Rathmann. Now they were turned toward home. Former winner Pat Flaherty spun, struck the mainstretch wall and was finished.

The last grueling laps slipped away. Rathmann cut down Thomson and took off after Ward in a final, furious bid, but Ward maintained his scorching speed. Some seventeen cars sat in the pits or back in Gasoline Alley, broken down, broken up or burned. Thirteen cars remained running with no hope of winning. As the afternoon wore on, clouds collected overhead, cool breezes blew across the dizzied and sunburned fans. The three leaders hurtled on toward their destinies.

In the final laps, Rathmann crept closer and closer, but Ward was out of reach. Shortly before three in the afternoon, after 3 hours and 40 minutes of fury, Ward slammed his Watson car across the start-finish line as the checkered flag fluttered at him. Just 23 seconds later, Rathmann rolled across, second for a third time, sorry and sagging. Then, Thomson came in.

As Ward coasted into Victory Lane, a wide smile splitting his broad, dirty face, his wife rushed at him. His dog leaped out of her arms at him and kissed him before the beauty queen could get to him. Ward was surrounded by Watson's crew and the rest of the Wilke team, by officials, by reporters and by photographers, all wishing the winner well, and the huge Borg-Warner Trophy was thrust into his sweaty hands.

At the victory dinner the next night, the winner's check for more than $100,000, from the purse of more than $300,000, was handed him. He said, "I don't know if I'm the best driver, but I know I had the best car. I think I'm a better driver than people believe I am, and with this car I think I can prove it."

There were those who wondered about Ward, but his win at Indy was only the beginning of a long run at the top for the veteran, who arrived late, but made the most of it when he got there. Along the title trail that summer, Rodger racked up victories on the pavement in Milwaukee and on the dirt at the state fair ovals in Indianapolis and DuQuoin to wrap up his first national driving championship.

No one wondered about car-builder Watson. His cars had finished first and second at Indy in 1959. They would finish first and second in the 1960 event, too. While working for Wilke, Watson was also working for himself. For 1960, he built four new cars. He kept one for Ward. Again, he sold another to the Rathmann team. He sold the others to others. His old cars were in the hands of still others. And still other car builders constructed new cars from plans obtained from Watson. One of these went to Eddie Sachs, another to Jim Hurtubise.

Sachs was in his fourth year at the 500. A fun-loving fellow, he was called "The Clown Prince of Racing." A mediocre driver early in his career, he had once washed dishes at a Speedway restaurant simply so he could stay close to a race that had refused him. He had become a competent driver because he had worked at it, wanting more than anything else in life to win at Indy.

On the opening day of qualification runs in 1960, Sachs sped through one lap at better than 147 miles per hour and averaged a record 146.5 for four laps to capture the pole position. It was, he enthused, the happiest day of his life. Eight days later, on the final day of time trials, rookie Hurtubise came within a tick of the stop watch of the fabled 150-mile-per-hour lap at Indy and surpassed the records of Sachs with a lap above 149 and an average above 149. Sachs was the first to congratulate him.

An admiring Mauri Rose stood off to one side and marveled, "Once in a while a fellow comes along with no worries. He doesn't feel like he's strapped in an electric chair. He's relaxed. He enjoys it. He loves it. It's fun for him. He doesn't know it's supposed to be tough."

But it was tough, and Hurtubise soon knew it. He led early, but his car collapsed late. The Sachs car caved in early. The race settled down to a renewed duel between Ward and Rathmann, with Thomson among the also-rans this time.

It was a wonderful race between the two veteran drivers in the two Watson streamliners. Watson's well-practiced pit crew serviced Ward swiftly on his stops, but he killed his car's engine on his first stop and fell a half-minute behind. By the midway mark he had cut his deficit in half. At 120 laps, Ward drew almost even with Rathmann. A few laps later, Rodger roared by his rival.

With 150 miles left, Ward seemed on his way to his second straight victory. He had come from far back to catch Rathmann. He seemed able to run faster. And he was ahead. But Rathmann clung grimly to Ward's tail. And when Ward tried to ease the pace to protect his car and rubber, Rathmann rolled around him. Ward picked up the pace right away to regain the lead. With $150 in bonus money for the leader of each lap, the lead had value. They circled the oval, tail-to-nose, far in front of the field, as the excitement in the ancient arena rose to a fiery pitch.

Each had one final stop scheduled, and at 147 laps both pitted. Never before had two competitors so close to one another pitted at the same time so late in this race. All eyes were riveted on the row inside the mainstretch as the crews worked feverishly to fuel the cars. Neither took time to replace tires. Ward roared out first, Rathmann right behind him.

With about 85 miles left, Rathmann ripped by Ward. Just 20 miles later, Ward roared past Rathmann to reclaim the lead. With 55 miles left, Rathmann dove under Ward to regain first. With 45 miles left, Ward whipped past to the top again. By now, the spectators were hollering loudly. The tires were wearing badly. The pace was taking its toll of the rubber. Conditions for the drivers were dangerous.

With 25 miles to go, Rathmann burst past Ward to lead again. It had become a dizzying duel and a test of courage. With 10 laps left, it was a sprint to the wire. For either to pit or to slow down would have been surrender, but for both men, not to seemed suicidal. As they charged toward the checker, their speeds increased from 142 to 143 to 144.

On the 196th lap, Ward drove by Rathmann once more. But one lap later, Rathmann drove deep into a corner and around Rodger and back into the lead, running the fastest lap ever run in traffic at the Speedway, above 146 miles per hour. Now, Ward's right front tire showed white, a warning that the outer rubber had worn off and what was left might blow and send him into a crash at any time. Ward eased off. Just a little. Just enough. Rathmann's right rear tire showed white, but he did not ease off.

It was, some said, a matter of Ward having won once and Rathmann never having won, of Ward maybe not wanting it as much as Rathmann. In any event, Rathmann maintained speed recklessly through the last three laps, his frayed tire held, he maintained his slight lead, and he charged under the checkered flag less than 13 seconds ahead of Ward. It was the second closest finish in this classic test. Only the race Wilbur Shaw had won from Ralph Hepburn almost a quarter-century earlier had been closer.

"It's tough to finish second when you know you have a car that can finish first, but it's better to finish on the track than in the hospital," a weary Ward sighed.

Rathmann, smiling as his crew and the crowd congratulated him, said, "I finished second here three times and I was going to finish first here this time if I had to risk everything for it."

Winning was worth $110,000 for Rathmann's team. For the second straight year, the difference between second and first came to close to $50,000. Now, each had won and lost the lion's share in spectacular races.

Their dramatic duels had increased interest in this classic contest enormously. The race-day crowd had climbed to close to 300,000 persons. The race-day purse had risen to almost $370,000, four times that of the first year of Tony Hulman's reign fifteen years earlier. But it had only begun its rise. The following year, it would reach $400,000. Three years later, it would reach half-a-million dollars. And it would continue to rise at about $100,000 a year as the crowds continued to increase.

But if Rathmann had been the hungrier driver in 1960, the fat purse he picked up seemed to ease his appetite. He would run three more races at Indianapolis, but never again would he be a contender in the classic. After fourteen 500's he would drift into retirement without ever being able to admit it officially. He had compiled a remarkable record at the Speedway, but would not join the exclusive ranks of those who won this great race more than once.

Meanwhile, Ward was arriving at a late peak in his profession and still longed for riches and glory. Watson's cars would be competitive every year. Ward realized that with conservative tactics he could continually run with the leaders and win if their cars gave out. "I had been around a while and I had come to see that to finish first, you have to finish. The higher you finished, the more money you made, but you had to finish. That's a lesson the kids still had to learn."

No longer a cocky kid himself, he was confronted with kids with ability coming up. One was A. J. Foyt, a tough Texan of twenty-six who was ready when he arrived for his fourth 500 in 1961.

The winds of change were whirling around the ancient track at this time. An American Grand Prix driver, Dan Gurney, had talked Australian Jack Brabham into entering one of the little, lightweight, rear-engined European racers in this greatest of American races, and he had talked Briton Colin Chapman into making the trip to take in the spectacle. The car was underpowered and not competitive, but its potential was impressive as Brabham placed it ninth.

However, Watson's roadsters—fifteen feet long, three feet wide, three feet high, 1,600 pounds pulled by an Offie engine from the front, remained dominant, filling half the spots in the starting field. Sachs put one on the pole. Hurtubise put another in the front row.

Ward put one in the second row. Parnelli Jones, a brilliant rookie, put another in the second row. Foyt put one in the third row.

"As a team member, I hate to be beaten by one of my own cars," Watson said, smiling. "But as a car builder, I have to be proud to see them do so well. I can be beaten, but I can't lose." Meanwhile, Wilke, the sponsor who supported Watson's team, grumbled about it angrily, but to no avail.

Johnny Thomson had been killed in a crash on a dirt track in a race at Allentown, Pennsylvania, the previous summer. Tony Bettenhausen had just been killed in a crash in practice for this Indy renewal. At forty, Rodger Ward endured to face the challenge of rising youngsters. "Suddenly, I'm the establishment," he laughed.

Hurtubise led, then his car cracked. Jones led, then his car cracked. Foyt and Sachs dueled for the lead, with Ward stalking them, waiting for their cars to crack. They didn't. In the late stages each had to make an emergency pit stop. Sachs took the lead as Foyt stopped for fuel. Then Foyt took the lead as Sachs stopped to replace a worn tire. Foyt finished first, with Sachs second after a spectacular duel. Ward finished third.

The canny, conservative Ward was winning two or three 100-milers on the one-mile ovals of the championship trail annually. Foyt won three of these in 1961 and with his first Indianapolis victory wound up with enough points to take his first national driving title. "It is time for someone else to take over at the top," he growled.

"I'll let him know when it's time," Ward wisecracked.

A feud comparable to those involving Milton and Murphy, Meyer and Shaw, had begun to build.

The kids were coming, but the old pro was far from finished.

In 1962 Parnelli Jones prodded a turnout of more than 100,000 persons into hysteria on the opening day of time trials by flying through four consecutive laps at faster than 150 miles per hour, bursting through the barrier brilliantly. But Ward qualified second fastest. On race day, P.J. and A.J. flew in front, but at 175 miles a wheel flew off Foyt's car, sidelining him; then at 300 miles the brakes gave out in Jones's car, and he lost the lead.

Ward came into the lead. Jones drove daringly without brakes, but he could not keep up and kept falling farther and farther back. Sachs, having had his troubles in qualifying and having started far back, drove daringly, too, and kept coming on, but poor work in his pits stymied him. Ward proceeded smoothly to the finish, followed in by a teammate in a sister car, Len Sutton. It was the second one-two finish for the Three W's (Ward, Watson and Wilke) and the fourth straight win for a Watson car.

Sachs had run the fastest race on the track, five seconds faster than Ward. But Eddie's crew had taken 87 seconds to service him, 25 seconds more than Watson's smooth crew had required to care for Ward, so Sachs had finished 20 seconds behind Ward.

"The race was won in the pits," the disappointed Sachs sighed.

"Mine was lost in the pits," Foyt fumed. A member of his crew had neglected to tighten a wheel. Losing it, Foyt had lost the race and almost his life. "I'll be back," he growled, a bigger Bill Vukovich.

"I'll be back, too, buddy," the sophomore Jones said, smiling sadly. He took a bent ten-cent piece of metal from sponsor Agajanian's hands and displayed it. "It broke. It beat us," he said.

Ward said, "You push metal too hard, it breaks just like anything else. You don't do the job in the pits, you lose your chance on the track. The driver drives, but the team wins. You put it all together right, and with a little luck you win."

The sixth man to win this hard race more than once, he proved a proud, but gracious winner. He admitted, "If nothing happened, there's no way I could win. No way. But something usually happens, and if you're in the right place at the right time you can take advantage of it."

Shrugging, a big grin creasing his greasy face, he said, "I ran smart and they ran unlucky. I'll take it anyway I can get it. Now I've done something few men have ever done. No one ever expected me to be the kind of man to do it. My life has always been up and down. It's nice to be up on top."

He was with Watson and Wilke, but almost alone and lonely there. Absent from Victory Circle was his wife, Jo. They had come apart. His parents were there. His grown sons, too. One of them, David, looked around and said, "You know there's a lot of disappointment here. There were thirty-two other drivers trying just as hard as my dad to win, and you have to feel sorry for them."

Rodger Ward observed, "It is a difficult life. It's hard on a wife. She worries while her husband drives. He risks his life every race he runs. It is hard on a family. But it's something we have to do. It's as if we were driven to it. And it has its rewards."

The purse was $462,000. Ward won $124,500, Sutton $44,500, Jones $33,000.

Through the rest of that summer, Ward and Foyt each won three races of from 100 to 200 miles on the short tracks of the title trail, but with the bundle of points from Indy, Rodger captured his second national driving crown. The paths of the two crossed at track after track, but they seldom spoke to one another.

The fiery Foyt said, "There's no reason we have to be friends. He's a great driver. I don't deny that. But I beat him out before and I can do it again. I think he's been on top long enough. I think it's time for me to be on top."

Ward said, "I figure Foyt is the man to beat. He's a very fine driver and he could become the greatest. But Jones is tough to beat, too, a great talent who could become great, too. I'm not ready to step aside yet.

"Foyt's a nice kid, really. He's just young and hot-tempered and he sometimes speaks before he thinks. I don't think he really dislikes me, it's just that I've been on top and he's coming up and it's only natural for him to pick on me."

In 1963, it was Parnelli's turn. His Watson-built Agajanian Special led most of the way. Colin Chapman had entered two rear-engined European lightweights, Lotus-Fords, for Scot Jim Clark and American Dan Gurney. Clark put a lot of pressure on Jones. When Parnelli's oil tank cracked, he could have been black-flagged off the track for spilling the slippery liquid, but he was not. He finished first, with Clark second.

Foyt finished far back, in third place, with a car that had handled horribly. Ward, recovering from a broken back suffered in a sports car crackup in Riverside, California, the previous October, finished fourth. Sachs threw a wheel and finished among the also-rans. Having slid in oil, he was angered. Later, he exchanged punches with Parnelli.

A savage season had taken the travelers into the 1963 Indy 500. Five drivers had left their lives along the side of the title trail, while Ward almost lost his during a detour. He said, "My steering and brakes went out at a hundred miles per hour. I went off a track and into a field. I turned over twice. The car was wrecked. I was hurt, but not beyond repair. I have scars on my body, but not on my mind."

He had a new bride, a young beauty queen. "I want to show her the old man still has a little left in him," he laughed. "I didn't have the best car at Indianapolis this time. If I'd had a better car, I'd have done better. I hope to have a better car next year. Watson has worked wonders before, maybe he can again. But Watson may have to change his ways. These new cars may be the way to go now."

A flood of the little lightweights had descended on Indy, and while Clark had not won with his, he had come close enough to throw a scare into the establishment. They feared these cars, which were low-slung and fragile. They hated the thought of junking the equipment they had developed at great expense over a great many years. But the new cars handled better. Their rear engines functioned better. With improvement based on experience gained at Indianapolis, the new cars could whip the old ones.

Some of the establishment stubbornly refused to go to the new cars, which, after all, had not yet won here. Foyt refused, despite the urging of his master mechanic, George Bignotti. Jones refused. Andy Granatelli still was trying with new versions of the old Novis, one driven by Jim Hurtubise. But Ward went over to the new cars. Sachs went into one. Clark and Gurney were back with new ones. Speed king Mickey Thompson was trying the race with sports-car-styled rear-engine machines, one to be driven by young Dave MacDonald.

A third of the entries and a third of the qualifiers for the 1964 Indy 500 were rear-engine lightweights. Clark put his on the pole with new record speeds of close to 160 miles per hour. Young Bobby Marshman and Ward put others into the front row. Jones and Foyt settled for second-row spots. Sachs, struggling to master his new machine, lost control and crashed into a wall. He stayed up all night while his crew repaired the car and got it into the field on the second day of trials, far back in seventeenth place, right behind MacDonald.

On race day the green flag was unfurled and the cars charged away, Clark in the lead. As Clark crossed the finish line at the end of his second lap, hell erupted behind him. MacDonald lost control, rammed a wall and came to rest in flames. Sachs, driving right behind him, had no time to avoid him and hit right into him, exploding into flames, too. Other drivers steered blindly through the black smoke. For the second time in its history, the race was halted. The first time had been because of rain. This time, tragedy. Both drivers died.

When the race resumed, Marshman wrestled the lead away from Clark and was far in front at 100 miles when his car gave out. Clark then resumed in the lead, but his tires came apart, setting up a vibration that broke the car's rear end and sent him out of control into the infield and out of the race. Jones then dueled Foyt for the lead until his car exploded in the pits while being refueled.

Foyt fell into the lead, far in front. Ward waited for Foyt to fall out, but he did not. Foyt finished first for the second time, while Ward finished well behind, second for the second time.

Ward had finished first, second, third, first, fourth, and second

in consecutive 500's, by far the finest record for six successive
races ever recorded at Indianapolis. He did not know it then, but
his time at the top had ended at last.

He sat in a coffee shop and discussed his life at the top in this
most dangerous of sports.

"I have had my close calls," he sighed. "I was pinned beneath
my car, not seriously hurt, but helpless when Vukie crashed to his
death. I couldn't help causing that accident. It was not my mistake, it was the car's, but I felt bad about it. I was lucky to get
out of it alive. I was lucky to escape from Riverside alive. I've
seen many of my friends killed driving. I came close to being
killed many times. You have to believe death can't happen to you,
however. This comes from having confidence in yourself.

"All good drivers have great egos. They have to believe they
can do this difficult and dangerous thing better and safer than
anyone else, or they'd never go near a racing car. We all get afraid
sometimes. I do. Not before a race. Not during a race. Not even
during an accident. But when an accident is over, when you think
about it. You wonder how you survived. But it passes. It's something you have to live with.

"When someone like Sachs and MacDonald die in a race, it
really shakes you up. You hate it. Frankly, you try to put it out
of your mind. It's hard, but you don't want to think about it. If
you thought about it intelligently you'd probably quit the profession. Even if you're one of the lucky ones who lives, I don't
know what makes up for losing friends and rivals. You have to
have a very hard crust."

A wistful smile spread over Ward's round face. He looked down
at his strong hands. "No one ever made anyone drive. We've all
gone into this thing of our own free wills. Of course, it's depress-
ing when a friend dies. I was close to Bettenhausen. I thought of
quitting when he died. But Tony wouldn't have wanted me to
quit. I wouldn't have wanted him to quit if I'd died. Most of us
love every moment we have in racing. I wouldn't trade the thrills

and satisfaction I've had in my racing career for any longer, safer life I might have led.

"We're set apart from other people, racing drivers, so we're more sympathetic to one another than men in most professions. We'll do anything to win on a racetrack, but we're very close off the track. Oh, I'm not close to Foyt. We're rivals and have become enemies of a sort. But most of us are close. We're members of a very exclusive fraternity. We do something others wouldn't dare do. It's a very special thing we do. I want to do it as long as I can do it well."

He was no longer young. He wouldn't admit it, but he was worried he had slowed down and lost his daring.

He said, "In racing, just as in any sport, it's the fellow who makes the fewest mistakes who usually wins. In racing, you usually can't afford too many mistakes and still survive. I made a lot of mistakes while I was learning to race, as many as anyone ever made. I don't make many anymore. I used to think speed alone won races. I used to think you had to lead every lap. Now I know the only lead that counts is the one at the end of the last lap.

"No one ever wins the 500. Thirty-two drivers lose it. I'm not physically what I was ten years ago, but I'm much more mentally. I may still be able to outsmart the kids. If they'll lose it to me, I'll take it. Three times is the most times anyone ever won this race. It's hard enough to win it even once. Many great ones never won one. I've won two. I'd like to have won three before I retire. Foyt wants three, too. He's younger than I am. He's not as close to retirement as I am. He hasn't felt all the things I've felt in this sport.

"It's a cruel sport, but a great sport. I've been considered a sort of spokesman for American auto racing. When I talk about it, I emphasize the good that's in it. But there is a bad side of it, too. I'm finding it harder and harder not to see that side of it these days," he admitted.

Foyt won ten races in 1964. Ward didn't win any. Foyt passed Ward in championship race victories, 27 to 25. Foyt passed Ward in national titles, 3 to 2.

In 1965, Ward took a new rear-engine lightweight built by Watson onto the Speedway and could not get it up to competitive speed. Each driver is allowed three chances to qualify each car. Ward took two of his chances on the opening day of time trials and was waved off as too slow both times. In Ward's first 500 when he was twenty-nine it took only a little more than 130 miles per hour to make the race. Now he was forty-three and the cars were going 25 to 30 miles per hour faster.

As qualifying and practice went on, and Watson and Ward worked desperately to become competitive with the car, others looked with sympathy at these falling heroes who had dominated this hard place so long.

During the week, someone asked Ward what was wrong. "Everyone's asking me what's wrong. If I knew, I'd do something about it, wouldn't I?" the usually pleasant veteran snapped harshly. Then he felt bad about it. Guiltily, he smiled, put his arm around the one who asked the question, and sighed, "I wish I knew."

On the third of the four qualifying days, while warming up before attempting his final trial run, Ward brushed an outside wall, spun, slid 500 feet and smacked the inside wall, flattening his car's nose and ripping off a wheel, then slid 200 feet back into the infield. He was shaken, but unhurt, and he walked slowly back to his garage.

Watson patted him on the back. "Ward, you're fired," he said, joking with a thin smile. Then they went to work to repair the car.

They worked all night and most of the final day of qualifying. With one hour to go, Ward sat in the repaired car, waiting to go onto the track and talking about the baby daughter who had just been born to him and his young wife. One of his two sons stood by his side. When it was Rodger's time to go out, the son shook his head hopefully and waved him away. Ward needed something close to 154 to make the starting field. He got a high 153, but missed by one tenth of one second. You can't count that fast.

After fourteen consecutive years in the race, he was out. He parked in the pits and sat there with his head down for a long time while photographers popped flashbulbs at him. Then he got out of his car and sat on a pit wall, slumped over, his elbows on his knees, his hands rubbing together, staring at the ground, his eyes hidden behind sunglasses.

A photographer asked him to get back into the car for more pictures. Shrugging, Ward did so. Then, when he began to get out again, another photographer asked him to hold it for "just one more." Ward said, "Aw, come on, what the hell," and got out.

Watson and others tried to console him. Ward said, "Maybe I shouldn't be in this thing anymore." He shrugged his shoulders, turned and walked away. Watson stood quietly, watching him.

The race that year was won by Jim Clark, an old hand with the new cars.

The next year, 1966, Ward returned with a new Watson car. He won the twenty-sixth title trail event of his career at Trenton. At Indy, he was first out in time trials and he averaged 159 miles an hour, which he knew would not be nearly good enough to capture the pole position, which he never had won, but he hoped it would be good enough to get him into the race.

He said, "I'll settle for it. I'm just glad to be back in it." Some felt that's all he wanted to do, make the race one last time, and retire from within it, not from the outside.

He did not drive the race hard. He was far back after 185 miles when he pulled into the pits, parked, and shut his engine off. His crew seemed stunned.

"What's wrong?" Watson asked.

"Everything's wrong," Ward said.

He got out of the car, took off his helmet, put it in the cockpit, and walked away, head lowered. No one said anything to him, but some patted him on the back as he passed.

Graham Hill, another Grand Prix driver, drove to the win that year the Ward way, winding up in front after the front-runners folded.

At the victory banquet, Rodger Ward stepped forward, took the microphone and said, "Years ago, I told myself if it ever stopped being fun, I'd quit." He paused as the gathering hushed. He began to cry and as he resumed, his voice choked in his throat. "Yesterday wasn't fun anymore," he said. With great effort, he added, simply, "Thank you." Then he waved and stumbled back to his chair, where he sat and wept unashamedly. Some wept with him. The crowd stood and applauded him for a long time.

He had many businesses, but they went bad. He went to work for the new Ontario Motor Speedway, but the track had troubles and cut its staff and him from it. He'd made a lot of money and spent a lot. He'd lived high and lost in married life. "I have no complaints about the life I've led," he said. "I've lived it as best I could. I've had a lot of fun. I hope to have a lot more."

He probably was one of the four or five greatest American race drivers of all time, as well as one of the four or five finest Indianapolis 500 champions. He remains an exclusive member of the fraternity of nine men who have won this great test more than once, and his career record is outstanding. He was to see Foyt go on to win a third Indianapolis 500, as well as the Pennsylvania and California 500's. He was to see Foyt go far past his total of 26 championship trail triumphs. Mario Andretti was to surpass it, too. Others threatened it. But in the middle 1970's, his total remained the third highest in history.

Almost ten years after he retired, Ward was racing again, driving stock cars in minor-league events on small tracks around southern California. "I had my time in the big time," he smiled. "I was in the majors. I don't mind the minors. It's cars. It's racing. There's money to be made. It spends the same as the Indianapolis dollar," he said.

"Could I still run with Foyt? Oh, I don't even think about it. He looks like he's going on forever. If he can get his fourth at Indy, fine, If he can, he'll have earned it. No man ever has done it. If he does it, I'll applaud him for it.

"I have no hard feelings about Foyt. We live in different worlds now. But he's still not as old as I was when I packed it in at Indy. His time will come, too. I may not be racing at Indy anymore, but I'm still racing. I'll tell you," he said, smiling wistfully, "I missed it a lot. It feels good to be back in it, even a little, just for fun. It gets in your blood, you know."

7   *A. J. Foyt*

1961, 1964, 1967

This was 1961, the golden anniversary celebration of the first Indianapolis 500.

Reborn from winter to spring, this warm, homely city in the midst of the midwestern farming community had stirred to full life, its hotels and motels packed, its restaurants and taverns crowded. There had been parties and parades. The sense of excitement had been rising.

Almost a million persons had purchased tickets to see the practice sessions, qualifying runs, and the race itself throughout this long month of May. The day and night before the race, cars were lined up for miles along 16th Street, waiting for the track to open.

This was the infield crowd. The people sweated in the day's heat and shivered in the night's cold—playing cards, dancing to music from transistorized radios, huddling around bonfires in the gutter, sleeping restlessly, waiting. Their cars and campers and trucks were their homes.

Shortly before dawn on Memorial Day there was a mock bomb burst, the gates were thrown open, and the vehicles, headlights peering through the gloom, raced into the infield in search of choice locations along the rails.

126

They used to erect scaffoldings atop their cars until one year one collapsed, killing some and injuring others, and they were banned. Now they put chairs on their cars. They pitch tents and throw blankets on the ground. If it has rained, they make a home in the mud. And renew their wait, drinking beer, eating chicken and raising hell.

Later in the morning, the last of the awesome race-day crowd of more than 300,000 persons had come from all across the country to fill the sprawling stands, watching the prerace pageantry of marching bands and old race cars, of beauty queens and visiting celebrities circling the 2½-mile oval.

Only those in the $55 penthouse seats high above the track can see most of the track. Most of the fans can see only a little of it. Some will see none of the race at all. For some, just being there is enough. It is a happening.

Eighty $50,000 cars were entered in quest of the thirty-three starting spots and nearly a half-million dollars in prizes. But it is more than money that attracts the daring drivers. Jimmy Bryan once said, "If you never win another dollar in racing the rest of your life, you will still be someone if you have won this race. You will have won the Indianapolis 500. You will always be known for that. When you're old and tired and scared and ready to die, you will still be someone who once won the 500."

So the teams had worked and waited eleven months since the last race for this one. Through the long month of May they pushed themselves to the ragged edge of disaster in pursuit of their passion.

Eddie Sachs said, "I think of Indianapolis every day of the year, every hour of the day, and when I sleep, too. Everything I ever wanted in my life I found inside the walls of the Indianapolis Motor Speedway. I love it all, from the first to the last day in May. On the morning of the race, if you told me my house had burned down, I'd say, 'So what?' The moment that race starts is always the greatest moment of my life. The day I win that race it will be as if my life has ended. There is nothing more I could want out of life."

The cars were pushed onto the track in their eleven rows of three. They were silent, waiting to be called to life. The drivers pulled on their crash helmets and strapped themselves into the cockpits. The Purdue band played "On the Banks of the Wabash." A singer sang "Back Home Again in Indiana." The national anthem was presented. Bombs burst and brightly colored balloons were released into the spring sky. And into a sudden hush, Tony Hulman said, "Gentlemen . . . start your en-gines!" And as the crews stirred the powerplants to roaring life, Sachs, sitting in his roadster on the pole, crossed himself and started to cry.

Right behind him, in the second row, sat old Rodger Ward, the former winner, the playboy professional. He said of this moment, "I feel the excitement. It presses in on me. But I know what I have to do. I have been here before. I have confidence in my car and myself. I feel I have a chance if all goes well."

In the third row, sat young A. J. Foyt, the defending national champion. He said of this time, "I am relaxed and ready. This is what I have been waiting for. This is what I have been working for. I don't have to put up with the other people now. I am alone now. I am at home in the cockpit of a car. I know I can do this damn thing."

No one else knows it yet, but he did. He was a tough young Texan, twenty-six years old out of Houston. Husky and handsome, he emerged from the savage sprint-car circuits of the Southwest to challenge the championship trail in 1956. He won his first championship trail event in 1960. In fact, he won four of the last six events to earn his first national driving title. But he'd had little luck at Indianapolis. His first 500, in 1958, he drove through a first-lap accident that crippled seven cars and killed driver Pat O'Connor, and drove well for 350 miles until he slid out on an oil slick. The following year, he drove the full 500 miles and finished tenth. In 1960, his car had given out at 235 miles. In 1961, he was back, in his best car yet, beautifully prepared by George Big-notti.

Some racing people said the powerful prodigy pushed his cars past their limits. The burly brawler denied it. "I drive them hard enough to win. I don't ask anything of them they're not supposed to do," he snapped.

The cars pulled away and slipped into their starting slots, circling the track slowly on their warmup laps. After two laps, the pace car accelerated ahead and pulled off into the pits. The cars picked up speed as they moved toward the starting line. The green flag was unfurled in front of them and they charged in a frightening tight tangle of traffic into the first turn with a deafening roar. They started to string out as they surged through a short chute into the second turn, through it, down the backstretch, into the third turn, through the second chute, into the fourth turn, and down the homestretch again in less than one minute.

There is nothing in sports quite like the start of the 500. It sets your senses on edge. You find it hard to breathe. The first lap is the worst one. It is the most dangerous one. This time, they were through it, safely. But one car had already broken down.

Jim Hurtubise led through 36 laps, but then his engine started to sputter and he limped into the pits, defeated. Defending champion Jim Rathmann took the lead, trailed closely by Ward and Sachs. Then the rookie Parnelli Jones passed Sachs, Ward and Rathmann within one lap to charge to the front. Jones held the lead, lap after lap. He held it as Rathmann turned into the pits with a sick engine and got out of his car, dethroned. He held it as Don Davis crashed on the mainstretch, got out in a daze, and began to walk across the track, five cars crashing in a skidding scramble to miss him. Somehow, no one was hurt and Jones picked his way through the debris and continued to lead.

Jones held the lead while Len Sutton spun out. He held it even after a piece of metal came off the track to gash his head and fill his cockpit with blood. He held it until his engine suddenly went sour and he started to lose speed no matter how hard he accelerated. First, former winner Troy Ruttman went past him. Then Foyt. Then Sachs. Then Ward. Then Foyt went past Ruttman. Soon, Ruttman limped into the pits, his car's components crippled. Now the race was among Foyt, Sachs and Ward. They swapped the lead back and forth under a broiling sun, dizzying the excited spectators.

With 125 miles left, Sachs, Ward and Foyt each made his last scheduled pit stop in turn. When these stops were done, Ward led, with Foyt second and Sachs third, but they were running in a pack. Then Ward's car caved in. The strain had cracked its chassis, it began to wobble, and he had to slow to stay on the track. Foyt and Sachs pulled away from him. Then Foyt began to pull away from Sachs. He built his lead to six seconds, seven, eight, and he seemed well on his way to winning.

Then, as Foyt went past his pits with 50 miles to go, he saw a sign held aloft by his crew at the pit wall. It said simply, "Fuel Low." He could not believe it. He should have gotten sufficient fuel to finish the race at his last pit stop. But, he had not. His fueling apparatus had malfunctioned. He was running in front, but running dry. He had no choice but to pit for enough fuel to finish the race. It was not a matter of braving it on a bad tire. It was not a matter of bravery at all. If he did not stop, he would not finish. If he stopped, it was likely to finish his hopes of finishing first, but he had no choice.

Many had seen the sign. Sachs's crew had surged to the pit wall, urging him on. The fans had come to their feet, watching the drama unfold in front of them. Finally, Foyt's pit crew signaled him, "Come In." Resignedly, he went into the pits with only 25 miles left to run. Hurriedly, fuel was pumped into his tank and he was pushed away. Before he could get back on the track, however, Sachs shot past him and into the lead. Before Foyt could regain his speed, Sachs had pulled in front by 15 seconds. Foyt launched a last desperate drive to cut down the leader, but Sachs was too far in front.

As the last laps unfurled under Sachs, he started to smile broadly and wave at his excited sponsor, Al Dean, and mechanic, Clint Brawner, in the pits, and at the crowd. In the stands, his wife, Nance, was crying happily, and counting off the laps—nine, eight, seven. An attendant came to escort her to Victory Lane. Superstitiously, she refused. She would not budge before Eddie had wrapped up this victory he wanted so much. Tears were streaming down her face as she watched Eddie come by each time—six laps, five . . .

At that moment, Eddie Sachs felt his car lurch. Shocked sick, he looked back to see the rubber peeling off his right rear tire. As he rolled past his pit, there was a sudden commotion. His crew saw it, too. The announcer screamed, "Something's going on in Sachs's pit. Something may be wrong with Sachs's car!" Nance Sachs grew faint and the color drained from her face. Her hands fluttered helplessly. George Bignotti jumped up and down in Foyt's pit and began to wave A.J. on harder. The crowd was standing as though in shock. No one could believe this race could so suddenly turn upside down again. But it could.

Sachs had seconds to make the most critical decision of his life. If he went on, his tire might hold and he would then win this race he had dedicated his life to winning. But if his tire blew out, he not only would lose the race, but might lose his life. If he stopped for a new tire, he could save second place and live to try another time. Suddenly, as he hurtled into the mainstretch with three laps left, he swerved into the pits. In the stands, his wife cried, "Oh, no, Eddie, no." His crew frantically fell on his car, replacing the tire, shoving him away. As he left, a crewman fell to his knees and in frustration hurled a hammer after him.

As Sachs reached the exit from the pits, a startled Foyt flew past and back into the lead. Sachs gunned onto the track, accelerated to top speed, and set out in pursuit. But it was hopeless, unless Foyt ran out of fuel. Even Foyt did not know how much fuel he had gotten in his hurried stop. He had little left, but he hurtled on. Two laps left. One lap. No laps. Foyt sped under the checkered flag as his fuel tank ran dry. Eight seconds later, Sachs came across, the second closest runnerup in Speedway history.

In Victory Lane, Foyt was enveloped in a great crush of excitement, congratulated, kissed, slapped happily. Sachs pulled to a stop and walked toward this ring of joy. He stood on the perimeter of madness, smiling sadly, looking down wistfully, scuffing his foot in the dirt. He went to his wife who had come tearfully to the fence parting the fans from the competitors. She asked him if he'd had to stop. He smiled wistfully and said, yes, he'd had to stop. Reporters got to him. He said, "It is better to be second than to be dead." And walked away, his head hanging, his hopes dead.

"Racing luck," Foyt said of his first 500 triumph. Would he have gambled and gone on had he been in Sachs's place? "I'd have gone on," he said. "You don't get that many chances to win this one. You take a chance every time you take the track. What's one more chance. But we make our own decisions out there. I wasn't in Eddie's place. I didn't see his tire. I can't say for sure what I'd have done, but I think I'd have gone on."

And now? "I'm going on," Foyt grinned. "This is just one. I want to win another one. And one after that. I want to keep on winning. I want to race the rest of my life. It is all I ever wanted to do with my life."

Anthony Joseph Foyt, Jr., born in January, 1935, was hooked early on the narcotic of racing. His father, a former race driver and mechanic, ran a garage that catered to racers. When he was three years old his father gave him a blood-red miniature racer. "I thought the car was the most beautiful thing there ever was," A.J. recalls. He took to it as though he had been born in it. At six, he was driving it in exhibitions between races at a local track. At eleven, he took a midget car that his parents had left behind while they went to the races, and tore up the backyard with it until it caught fire. He put the fire out and went to bed. His father accepted it. "I could see it was what he had to do," the old man said.

A.J. learned to drive cars and motorcycles early. At seventeen, he quit school and began to race motorcycles. At eighteen, he began to race jalopies, old stock cars and new stock cars. Then he raced midget cars and sprint cars. He won a lot. And he was as fast with his fists as with his cars. A rival remembers, "He was too good for the other guys. He'd boil over when he got beat by any of them, and they'd boil over when he beat them. He was a wild man. He was fighting his way up." At twenty-three he headed for the Midwest and started to race sprint cars and championship cars. He kept on winning and fighting. He was confident to the point of cockiness, but he really was good, and as a result he got good rides. But it was a bad, dangerous school he attended.

"The early days are the most dangerous," Foyt once observed. "You run races that aren't real fast, but you run 'em as hard as you can. The tracks aren't real good, the cars aren't real good, and a lot of the drivers aren't real good. You get a bad guy in a bad car and you got a rough situation for the rest of the guys. Sprint-car racing probably is the most dangerous form of racing. They're the most high-powered cars you run on short tracks. I always liked sprint racing because I was always good at it. Sprint cars race on dirt tracks and I was always good on dirt. Racing dirt, on a short track, it's more the driver than the car, and I like that."

Today, with the sophisticated rear-engine cars racing at Indy, the road to Indy is often through sports-car ranks, in races run on fancy, paved tracks, but for many years the traditional trail to Indy was through sprint-car races on small, dangerous, dirt tracks, and this was the way A. J. Foyt went.

He moved up to the majors in 1956, joining the United States Auto Club and campaigning with midget cars, sprint cars and championship cars in USAC events. His first USAC victory was in May, 1957, in a 100-lap midget feature on a quarter-mile dirt track in Kansas City, Missouri. His first sprint-car victory was in April, 1960, when he won a 30-lap feature on a half-mile dirt track at Reading, Pennsylvania. His first championship car victory was in July, 1960, when he won a 100-mile contest on the mile dirt oval at DuQuoin, Illinois. That year he went on to win three more title events, accumulating enough points to win his first national driving crown.

For five years he had scraped up the cash to see the Indianapolis 500. He was the youngest driver in the starting field in his first 500 in 1958. He still was the youngest driver when he won his first 500 in 1961. He won three more races that year and his second national title. He was the youngest man ever to win Indy and the national title in the same season.

In 1962, Foyt won three of the first four races on the championship trail, but he lost the 500. He was the victim of an incredibly careless act when one of his crew neglected to tighten a wheel after a change during a pit stop. Foyt had just rolled away from the pits and was in the lead when the wheel flew off the car. Somehow, he succeeded in executing a safe stop, emerged in grimy disgust, cursed his crippled car, then ran a mile back to the pits, hoping for the chance to drive relief for another driver. In that race Ward won his second Indy victory.

An angry Foyt fired most of his pit crew. Late in the season he fired his chief mechanic, George Bignotti. Then he rehired him. Foyt was always firing and rehiring Bignotti. Both were brilliant, but both had big egos and they were always arguing.

Bignotti said, "Foyt is a brilliant driver and a brilliant mechanic, but you can't drive and be your own chief mechanic. He just can't leave his mechanic alone. He changes things around, then blames me when they don't work."

Foyt said, "The sponsor hires a mechanic and the mechanic hires a driver. The mechanic prepares the car, but the driver has to drive it. The driver takes all the risks. The driver shouldn't work for the mechanic, the mechanic should work for the driver. That's the way it has to be on my teams. If the sponsor doesn't like it, I'll get me another sponsor. When I have to do something, I want it done my way."

Even young, Foyt was hardheaded, a hard man. But he knew the way to win and wanted to win more than he wanted anything else in life. He hated to lose more than any man on tour, and none of them liked to lose. He was a gracious winner, but a bitter loser. In good times he was all smiles, spreading the credit around. In bad times he was sullen, unapproachable. The spotlight didn't warm him. Demands on his time turned him cold. He stuck close to his cars and his crews. He drove as often as he could. He drove forty to fifty races a year. He started to drive stock cars. He tried sports-car racing, winning the Nassau Trophy Race in the Bahamas. "If there's a race somewhere, I want in it," he said.

If he was in a race, he wanted to win it. The money didn't matter. He was beginning to make a lot of money, but he ran for small money as well as big. Once he entered a sprint-car race at Terre Haute. A big crowd was on hand, but it rained so hard the drivers refused to run. The promoter pleaded with Foyt to qualify, hoping it would encourage the others to follow. Foyt agreed. The muddy track held his speed down. The sun came out, drying and smoothing the track. Others qualified faster, bumping Foyt from the starting field. Angrily, Foyt paid the last-place qualifier for his position, took his unfamiliar car, and drove like a demon to pass everyone and win the race. Triumphant, he roared, "Lordy, but the boys are burned up."

It is competition, not cash, that inspires him. That same year, while warming up for a stock-car race in Milwaukee, he blew his engine in practice. Rather than stay on the sidelines, he took over an unfamiliar last-place car, started last, and won again. Once he entered an unimportant Indianapolis sprint-car race on an unfinished new oval only a few days before the 500. His sponsor did not dare protest. Parnelli Jones said that if a sponsor did protest, A.J. would just tell him to go to hell. Hearing this, A.J. happily agreed, "I reckon that's what I'd do."

In 1962, Ward parlayed his point-rich Indianapolis success into his second national title. Foyt didn't like Ward and he didn't like losing the title. That season and the next, he changed sponsors three times in search of the support and equipment he felt he needed to win. In 1963, he won five races to regain the national laurels, even though his car in the 500 was not sound and he had to struggle to finish third with it behind winner Parnelli Jones and runnerup Jim Clark. Foyt did not join in the tirade against Jones for running while spilling oil. "If they don't stop you, you don't stop," he said.

In 1964, Foyt hit his peak. He set records by winning seven straight championship races and ten in all, including his second 500, to gain a record fourth national title. The 500 was a hard-earned, but somewhat hollow triumph.

By that time the electricity of change had been generated at the Speedway. The new Grand Prix-style rear-engine lightweight cars were clearly the fastest and smoothest, if not the sturdiest and safest cars in the competition. Foyt was one of the old guard, reluctant to turn from the traditional front-engine heavyweights to the European entries. On the second lap of the 500 that year, Dave MacDonald crashed and exploded into flames and Eddie Sachs crashed into him to form a funeral pyre. The race had to be halted while the track was cleared. Foyt sat on the ground along-side his roadster and said, "I dread the day when I'll be driving one of those funny cars."

He could not keep up with them after the race resumed, but after the lightweights of Bobby Marshman and Jim Clark caved in, and after the heavyweight of Parnelli Jones exploded in the pits, Foyt's heavyweight held the lead and he went on to win by three miles over runnerup Rodger Ward. In Victory Lane, as his wife kissed his smiling, grease-smeared face, Foyt was handed an extra edition of the *Indianapolis News*, headlined in a hurry, "Foyt Winner in 500, Sachs, MacDonald Die." It was a bitter-sweet moment. To a friend, Foyt whispered, "You know, a few years ago, Sachsie should have kept going." He'd had his chance and he'd let it get away from him. He'd saved his life, but now he'd lost it here, anyway.

That morning, Sachs had said, "I used to want it for myself. Now I want it for my family. Someday, my son will stand in a school playground somewhere and he'll be able to say to the other kids, 'My daddy won the 500.' "

That afternoon, that was taken away from his son.

A few afternoons later, in a 100-mile championship race at Milwaukee, Ward, Foyt and Hurtubise were running one-two-three in a tight bunch midway in the event. The rear suspension in Ward's car snapped, the car swayed, and he slowed suddenly. Reacting instantly, Foyt cut his car hard to the right, narrowly avoiding Ward. At that instant, Hurtubise also cut right. The left front wheel of Hurtubise's car rode up over the axle of the right wheel of Foyt's car, and Hurtubise's machine sailed into the air and nosed down against an outer wall. The fuel tank burst and the car exploded in flames, shrapnel raining onto the track.

Hurtubise was extricated from the car and hurried to a hospital. It would be many months before he would recover. He would be scarred for life. One hand would be immobile. He had his choice which way it would be set permanently. He had it set in a curled position so he could curl it around a steering wheel. He would resume racing, though he would never realize his early promise.

Foyt had gone on to win the race.

Foyt sat in a motel and talked about living with death. He said, "It hurts when you lose friends. Hell, we got feelings like anyone else. A good guy goes and you want to park your car and chuck your helmet in the cockpit and walk away from it. But this is our business. Death and injury are part of the sport. Not as big a part as some want you to believe, but a part. We all live with it. We all know it can happen to us. We accept it because we want to race. We try not to make too many close friends. But you can't live with guys and not make friends."

In January, he was driving a stock-car race on the Riverside road-racing course near Los Angeles when his brakes failed. He was running at 140 miles per hour just behind cars driven by Junior Johnson and Marvin Panch as they entered a turn. Foyt had a fraction of a second to decide on a course of action. He knew that if he rammed either or both of those in front of him, he'd probably survive, but they might not. He didn't think he could get around them and stay on the track, but he figured he had to try. Later, he said, "You don't exactly reason it out. Hellamighty, there is no time for debate. If you've been doing this thing a while, you get the picture right away and react by instinct. You want to live, but if you live, you have to live with yourself."

He wrenched his steering wheel hard to the left and cut to the inside, trying to straighten out. He hung on the inner rim of the track for a long moment, then slid down and hurtled down the embankment, bouncing end over end, 100 feet high, 50 feet high, 20 feet high, before settling down in a steaming crumpled heap at the bottom of the gully. Fortunately, there was no fire. Rescue workers pried him from the bent metal and rushed him to a hospital. He had fractured bones in his back and one heel. Almost all of the skin had been scraped from his body.

Foyt was placed in a cast and lay flat on his back for several weeks. When the cast was cut off, he was strapped into a brace and permitted to walk a little with crutches. Three months after the accident, he limped into Atlanta Raceway to run another stock-car race. When he was asked what he was doing there in his condition, he stuffed his hands in a windbreaker, made a sour face, shrugged, asked, "Where else should I be?" and limped off. Another driver admitted, "He hurts so much he can't sleep nights, but he won't admit it."

One third of the way through the race, Foyt came charging up on Panch again when his throttle stuck. "I thought, 'Uh-oh, here we go again," he recalled later. This time, however, there was a way out on the high side. Foyt scraped to a stop safely along the wall. Disappointed, he walked back to the pits. Panch signaled that he was sick and needed relief. Foyt replaced him and went on to win the race.

The following month, still limping in pain, he was back at Indianapolis for the 1965 race. This time he had one of the new cars. He was practicing it at 160 miles per hour when a wheel broke off. He slid almost 1,000 feet out of control, backed the rear end into an outside wall, then shot across the track to pound the front end into an inside wall. Along the way, another wheel broke off, flew up and rolled across his helmet and shoulders. As the car plowed to a stop in the infield, Foyt jumped out. When the rescue crews reached him, he was circling the car, asking over and over, "Am I all right?" Calming himself, he said, "I told myself that this thing might catch fire, but it's not going to be Foyt that burns."

He had to go to a medical station to be examined. The doctor discovered to his amusement that A.J.'s pulse rate was already back to normal. Foyt said, "Hurry up, doc, I got to go back and get my car fixed up."

It was repaired in time for the first day of time trials. Early in the day Clark set new record speeds of 160.9 for one lap and 160.7 for four. He was still being applauded as Foyt rolled out to surpass his speeds with newer records of 161.9 for one lap and 161.2 for four to capture the pole position. As the spectators cheered him wildly, it was surprising to hear him announce sentimentally, "I'm glad to get the record back for America."

He was not able to win the 1965 race for America, however. His gearbox gave way just past the midway mark and Clark went on to win. Depressed, Foyt admitted, "Maybe it's time to quit." But he did not and went on that year to win five championship trail races, plus the Firecracker 500 at Daytona for the second straight year, against some of the best stock-car racers in one of the South's classic contests. However, young Mario Andretti placed high so consistently along the title trail that he edged out A.J. for the national championship.

Foyt, who has finished second six times, while winning the U.S. crown five times, stepped aside from season to season only grudgingly. If an Andretti had pushed past him one season, Foyt wanted to put him back in his place the next season. In his garage one day he said, "I got to get better because I don't want to get beat. I got to be the best, and I want always to be the best. Those hot kids are always coming at me. I'm king of the hill and they want to knock me off.

"It takes hard work to get to be king of the hill and harder work to stay on top. That's why I work so hard. I probably work harder than any other driver. They gripe about how hard they work, but that's a bunch of bull. Most of them don't work on the cars at all. They don't even hang around here when they're being worked on. When they're ready, they drive them. In my book, that makes them chauffeurs.

"I'm a driver. I don't want anyone doing anything to my cars I don't know about. I want to be there and I want to be working," he said.

Still brawling his way through life off the track, often at odds with USAC, sometimes threatened by suspensions, he remained his own man: "Winning, whooeee, that's what it's all about. There's nothing on earth like it. It makes me sick any time I lose. I blow off steam and people criticize me for it. But I'm human. I can get mad just like anybody else. Anybody gets in my way, I get mad," he said.

"To be a winner, to be successful, you have to pay attention to detail. I won't allow sloppy work in my garage or at the track. There is no room for errors either by the drivers or their crew. You're alone out there in the car. A mistake back in the garage or in the pit could end it all for you. I'm not anxious to hurry death along. Since I'm the one that has to go out there and drive the car and run the risks, I have the right to have things my way."

During the 1965 season Foyt finally fired Bignotti for the last time. He hired John Pouelson, who had been Parnelli Jones' mechanic. Before the season ended, Foyt fired Pouelson, too. Foyt became his own chief mechanic, hiring his father to captain his team. But 1966 was his worst year.

At Indianapolis he was involved in a first-lap crash that eliminated eleven cars from contention. As the cars skidded across the track on their bellies with wheels broken off and bounding around, Foyt slid to a stop, climbed a fence in front of the grandstand and hung there while fans laughed at his undignified act. He didn't laugh.

In 1966 he didn't win a big race all year. Bitter rival Rodger Ward had retired, but Foyt's newest challenger, Andretti, won his second straight national title. Englishman Graham Hill, a Grand Prix champion, won the 1966 500. He did not retire until 1975. Near the end of that year he was killed when the private plane he was piloting crashed.

Still, Foyt pressed on. He began to build his own cars, which he called Coyotes, and to field his own racing teams with the sort of strong sponsorship support his prestige commanded. And 1967 was a comeback campaign for Foyt.

This was the year Andy Granatelli brought a turbine-powered car to Indianapolis with Parnelli Jones as pilot. Foyt knew he could not outrun Jones in this smooth-handling, low and wide revolutionary racer, so he simply decided to outrun everyone else, and hope the turbine would not last. It was shrewd strategy. Jones led most of the way and was far in front near the finish, but with eight miles to go a ball-bearing broke in the gearbox and the turbine shuddered and died. Foyt heard the roar of the crowd and hurried on. Moments later he drove past his old foe, parked in the infield, to take the lead.

"All of a sudden, I had a third 500 victory in my hands, as many as any man has ever won," Foyt later recalled. "I had a funny feeling something would happen. It's not like me, but I got cautious all of a sudden." He swept around the track once, twice. As he drove into the final turn of the final lap, a five-car crackup occurred right in front of him. The track was covered by skidding cars. Wheels and metal rained like hailstones out of the skies. The crowd was on its feet in shock. Dust obscured the scene. Most figured Foyt had crashed or would. However A.J. coolly braked sharply, sought holes and picked his way through the chaos to come across under the checkered flag ahead of Al Unser and, in a sister Foyt team car, Joe Leonard.

The last man to win in one of the old front-engine heavyweights, he had become the first American to win in one of the new rear-engine lightweights. Goodyear had bankrolled him in a bid to end Firestone's tire supremacy at the Speedway and Foyt had come through.

The fourth man in history to win three victories in this classic contest, Foyt now wanted to be the first to win four. "I guess this puts me in exclusive company," he grinned as he accepted congratulations in a tumultuous Victory Lane. "Maybe I can now put myself out front all by myself."

A disappointed Jones retired. Ward had retired. Rathmann had retired. Bryan, who had won Foyt's first 500, was dead. Sachs was dead. Thomson was dead. Before the following 500, Clark would be killed. But Foyt went on. Twelve days after winning at Indianapolis for the third time, he teamed with Dan Gurney to win the most prestigious of European endurance races, the 24 Hours of LeMans. He and Graham Hill are the only drivers ever to have won both Indianapolis and LeMans.

Returning, he won four more events along the championship trail. Yet entering the season's final race, Foyt led Andretti by only a few points in contention for the national title. If Andretti did well, Foyt had to do well, too, to stay in front. The canny competitor arranged with friendly rivals to take over their cars in case his car failed him, so he could collect part of their points. He tangled in a turn with Al Miller and spun out of the event. He rushed back to the pits and beckoned in Jim Hurtubise, but just as A.J. jumped into the cockpit, the car stalled. He jumped out, signaled in Roger McCluskey, and took over his car. He finished fifth in the car. Andretti finished second but fell short by a few points of stopping Foyt from winning an unprecedented fifth national crown.

Andretti sighed and said, "He will do anything to win."

Parnelli Jones observed, "I was better than most because I would do more than most to win, but A.J. always was willing to do more than anyone."

Wistfully, Rodger Ward observed, "He is the best because he is smart as well as skilled. He will put himself in places on a racetrack others will not go. He is a charger who likes to lead and will get as far in front as he can in most races, but he has won the biggest race of all, Indianapolis, by playing a waiting game, by falling into the lead after others fell out of it. He is lucky, as well as good. That is a tough combination to beat."

In his first five years on the title trail, Foyt had won more championship races, twenty-seven, than Ward or anyone else ever in their entire careers. In his first ten years, he had won thirty-seven races and five national titles. The purse in his first 500 victory was $400,000. His team collected almost $120,000. The purse in his second was more than $500,000 and his team took home more than $150,000. The purse in his third was almost $750,000 and his team took in more than $170,000. Three times in his career he had earned more than $100,000 a year. One year, he earned more than $175,000. He had become the first driver in any form of racing to total more than a million dollars in winnings. He had invested his money wisely. He owned an automobile dealership and parts of assorted successful enterprises. If he never made another dime, he could live comfortably the rest of his life.

Foyt had married his teen-age sweetheart. He and Lucy had three healthy children. He had a lavish home in Houston and a vacation house on a lake. He owned assorted luxury cars, a speedboat, even his own airplane he flew himself. He had just about everything a man could want. He was in his early thirties and he still had his health. A husky, handsome fellow, his hair was thinning, but he was in the prime of his life. He admitted he regretted time taken away from his family. He confessed his family wanted him to retire. But he was not tempted by the soft life. All he wanted to do was work on cars and race them. "Everyone wants me to retire except me," he said. "I know the longer I drive, the greater the risks, but I'm no more worried about it than I ever was. If I retired, I don't know what I'd do with myself. Racing is my life. When I quit racing, it will be like ending my life."

So, he pursued his passion of becoming the first man ever to win a fourth at Indy. But it eluded him. In 1968, in practice, Mike Spence was killed in the crash of his turbocar and Bob Hurt was paralyzed in the crash of his car. Joe Leonard pushed the qualifying record above 170 miles per hour in another turbocar and led until nine laps were left, when his revolutionary car quit. Bobby Unser breezed to victory. Foyt's car collapsed before the race was half over.

Restrictions imposed on the turbocar then caused Granatelli to withdraw them and they faded from the scene. The rear-engine lightweights, their fuel tanks beefed up, had become safe and again became the dominant car at the track in 1969. Granatelli sponsored Andretti in one and Mario finally won one, giving the flamboyant fat man a long-sought triumph at Indy. Dan Gurney, building his own Eagles now, finished second for the second straight year. Foyt had captured the pole position for the second time in his career, but had dropped from contention while leading at the midway mark when his engine went sour. After 22 minutes in the pits, he resumed the race, running until flagged off at the finish, running just to run.

In 1970, Foyt led twice. He was running second and within reach of the lead late in the race when he tore up his gearbox wrenching his car away from an accident in front of him. He lost power and crawled the rest of the way.

In 1971, he started the season by winning the Daytona 500, the classic contest of the southern stock-car set. At Indianapolis his car ran all day, but it didn't run fast enough. Al Unser, driving for the team put together by Parnelli Jones, became the fourth driver to win Indianapolis two years in a row. Bignotti was the chief mechanic both times, which really got to Foyt, who finished third.

In 1972, Mark Donohue overcame A.J. after Foyt was finished at 150 miles with a sick engine. In 1973, a cruel race in which Art Pollard was killed, a race reduced to 133 laps by rain, Gordon Johncock brought Bignotti his sixth Indianapolis win, while Foyt was finished after 37 laps when his chassis came apart. And all this time, Foyt seldom was winning anywhere on the title trail. He won four times in 1968. He won once in 1969. He did not win even once in 1970. He won once in 1971. He did not win in 1972. Meanwhile, Bignotti was winning more than any mechanic in history. Veteran mechanic Watson was struggling, unable to successfully make the shift from the old cars to the new ones. Veteran mechanic Brawner was struggling. But Bignotti was winning.

"I don't know how many we'd have won if we'd have stayed together, but we would have won a lot. You can't win many being your own mechanic, building your own cars and driving them, too," Bignotti said. Others said it, too. Foyt was stubborn, they said. He could go into one of the good cars and win with one, but he had to build it himself, and he wasn't as good a builder as he was a driver. He wasn't a winner anymore, they said. He was past his prime. Foyt fumed. One of the few men ever to have won Indianapolis with a car he had constructed and prepared himself, he was a proud person who was convinced he could do it his way. By now he had taken over the Ford racing engine and renamed it the Foyt. He felt he could win not only with his own car but with his own engine.

"A lot of luck goes into racing," he said. "I've run into a string of hard luck. A lot of little things have gone wrong with my cars. Others are ahead of me, right now. But someone always has to be ahead. So Bignotti's ahead now. He's a good man. But I'll catch up. I'm building good cars and I'll get me one that's ahead of all the others. Just you wait and see. I can still win. I'm winning everywhere else except Indianapolis and the championship trail,

and those other wins count, too, you know. I'm far from finished."
He was, indeed, a long way from the end. He was winning elsewhere, winning on the stock-car trail whenever he had a competitive car.

He remained durable, this enduring giant. In 1972, USAC removed dirt-track races from the championship trail and set them
up in a short title trail of their own. At DuQuoin, Foyt's car caught
fire as he was departing the pits. Leaping from it, he was badly
burned, hurt his wrist, and tore an ankle up. He was in a knee-
length cast for a month, in a wheelchair for a while, then on
crutches.

By then, new Indianapolis-style tracks had been constructed to
host 500-mile events at Ontario, California, and Pocono, Pennsylvania, and when the California classic came up, Foyt limped into
it. By this time there were cars capable of qualifying at better than
200 miles per hour. Despite pain, Foyt qualified sixth fastest, but
his engine failed fast. Returning to the tour, he won the first dirt-
course crown.

Refusing to take time out for an operation, he returned home to
build a new Indianapolis car. It won for him at Trenton. After it
failed him at Indy in 1973, he won with it at Pocono. He sped past
old pal Roger McCluskey when Roger ran afoul of new and severe
restrictions on fuel and ran dry with only 60 miles left. For a happy
Foyt, it was his fourth victory in a 500 for Indianapolis cars.

His car failed him again at Ontario, but by then he felt he had
figured out the formula with which he could construct one that
would win for him.

In 1974, Foyt's new winged Coyote was the class of the California 500. The race had been moved up to March and Foyt's car
was by far the fastest in the field. He sped onto the pole with his
new wonder, five miles per hour faster than the next fastest car.
He captured a 100-mile qualifying event with it, too. He had constructed a streamlined speedster that frightened his rivals. "If
Foyt's new car doesn't break down, we can't beat him," Bobby

Unser admitted. However, it broke down with a severed oil line while far in front after only 50 miles, and Bobby did beat him.

Still, Foyt went to Indy hopefully. "I'm ahead of the others and they know it. They'll have to catch me if I can keep this thing together," he observed. He ran afoul of the wind and was kept from the pole by Peter Revson, who toured the course at 200. However, Revson never led the race. Foyt did twice. And then his engine lost power and his car was crippled. In ten tries, John Rutherford had not come close to capturing this classic. This time he had a top car and he won with it.

Foyt went on his way. He failed at Pocono. But he went on. Revson was killed overseas. His racing days were done. Foyt won at Trenton. He was winning again.

In 1975, Foyt's car remained the fastest at California. He captured the pole position. He won another 100-mile qualifying race. And this time he won the 500-mile race. No one could come close to him. He led 188 out of 200 laps, finished two miles in front of Bobby Unser, and pocketed $90,000. In the process, he recorded another first. He was the first driver to win all three championship trail 500's, "The Triple Crown" of the circuit. "That's an honor," he said. "But I don't think about those things much. I just want to win."

In the Trenton 200, he won his milestone fiftieth national championship victory, almost twice as many as the next man in line. "Is that all?" A.J. asked the press afterwards.

"And Indy?" he was asked.

"Well, Indy will be different," A.J. said.

"What will be different?"

"At Indy, I'll have a faster car," A.J. said, smiling.

And if he finally won his fourth at Indy, would he then retire?

"Oh, I dunno," A.J. said, grinning. "I might want my fifth, then."

He did not get his fourth. In his eighth try for it, he was betrayed by his desire to be better than the best, which he already was. Although he had a car that had become the best, at Indianapolis in 1975 he went into a new car which he thought would be better, and it betrayed him. It was neither faster nor stronger. All month he struggled with it, but he stubbornly stuck to it while parking his proven racer in the garage.

All the month of May, Gordon Johncock in George Bignotti's new Wildcat ran faster. On the opening day of qualifications, Foyt somehow flashed around at an average speed of almost 194 miles per hour to take the pole from Johncock, but on race day Johncock immediately leaped into the lead and held it for 20 miles until his engine went sour.

Foyt took over then, but Wally Dallenbach, coming from far back in twenty-first starting position in another of Bignotti's Wildcats, cut him down at 150 miles and commenced to pull far in front. Foyt fell farther and farther back, until he was behind not only Dallenbach, but also Johnny Rutherford and Bobby Unser.

This was his eighteenth Indianapolis 500, which was the record, all of them run consecutively. He started the race on the pole for the fourth time, tying the record of Rex Mays. By the time it was completed, he had finished 2,561 laps and 6,402½ miles in this classic contest, both new records, and had led these races for 445 laps and 1,112½ miles. But he did not lead it on the lap he wanted to most of all, the last one of the 1975 event.

Foyt fell behind in his new car even before he ran over wreckage in the late laps. Dallenbach's engine expired, and Bobby Unser beat out Johnny Rutherford in a run for the finish before a sudden downpour ended the race after 174 laps and 437½ miles.

Foyt skidded across under the checkered and red flags just ahead of Bobby Unser—but almost a lap back in third place. In bitter disappointment, he parked his Coyote, fled from the press, and presumably began to plot his strategy for the sixtieth Indianapolis 500 in 1976. First he headed for the hospital where he was treated for a sore hip. He had driven half the race sitting on a jagged piece of metal, which had torn loose in his cockpit.

He went on to win the Pennsylvania 500, the first to win it

twice. This gave him six 500-mile victories. The only 500 which eluded him in 1975 was Indy. He won seven races during the year, which gave him 54 championship circuit victories, and his sixth national title.

He had turned forty. His worth was estimated at $10 million. He had won more races in more different kinds of cars on more different kinds of tracks and he had won more titles than any driver in the history of racing. He was generally regarded as the greatest driver in the history of racing. He was a living legend, perhaps the toughest competitor any sport has seen. And he hated the thought of retirement, which was pressing in on him now.

In a moment of weakness he said he might retire. Then he denied it. "That was a bunch of malarkey," he snapped. "When I decide to retire, I'll just pull into the pits, jerk off my helmet, and tell everybody to go to hell."

The Unsers and the others were hammering at him, but he had not changed. He was still the King, even if others conspired to keep his crown from him.

8   *Al Unser*

1970, 1971

Bobby Unser

1968, 1975

It would be impossible for most of us and it is hard for many racing drivers, but it seems easy for Al Unser, driving a powerful, fragile car four times as fast as we are permitted to travel on the freeways, and in tight traffic, in close competition, for more money to be made in a single day than some of us will earn in our lifetime.

He denies that it is easy. He says, "If you're good, and I'm good, you make it look easy, but it's hard, and it gets harder, not easier, all the time."

Still, he is able to sleep soundly the night before big races. He puts away big breakfasts the morning of big races because he knows he will be busy at lunchtime. And he kids around with the other drivers just before they get into their racing cars.

He just gets in and goes. A few drivers tense up and turn away from the world, their eyes hiding secret thoughts just before they are imprisoned in what seems like a coffin to them. A few can't sleep and can't eat as race day approaches and can hardly talk as the time to take off arrives.

Most who do this thing well are comfortable in a race car and at home on a racetrack and look on racing as a high-paying, prestigious profession, and they go to work as easily as others go to school or to the office or to the factory. Few even think of death or injury unless some fool of a frightened reporter asks them about it. But few are as relaxed in this sport as is Al Unser.

He grew up with it, more than most. Many who do not love it look down on it and figure as fools those who do it, yet the number of sons of drivers who follow their fathers into this savage sport, even the sons of fathers who died driving, the number of brothers who enter into it, shows how those who are part of it feel about it. There really are a lot of them, such as Gary Bettenhausen's three sons, Bill Vukovich's son, Johnny Parsons's son, Duane Carter's son.

Al Unser's father, his father's brothers, his brothers, all have raced. An uncle and a brother were killed in crashes. Brother Jerry was killed in a crash at Indianapolis. But Al just gets in and goes and he has gone so well that he has won the Indianapolis 500 twice. Brother Bobby, his fiercest rival, has also won Indy twice. Bobby also won the California 500 once, beating out Al by three short seconds.

"You know I never thought about what else I might do in life," Al admits. "I really don't know what else I could do. I grew up in racing. I never thought about anything else. I do it well. I make good money at it, and I enjoy the life. It's very simple. Not easy, but not complicated. If you can get good men to put together good cars for you, you go the best you can with them.

"You run risks, but there are a lot of professions in which you run risks. You can get killed walking across a street or slipping in a bathtub. Most race drivers are fatalists. They figure when their number is up, it's up, no matter what they're doing. They could do something safer, but maybe it would be less fun, less exciting, less rewarding."

Brother Bobby adds, "You never know how long you'll live, so the thing is to make the most of it while you can. If you're not cut out to be a race driver, you won't be one. You can't talk a man into it. It would scare most people to death just trying it once. If it scares you, you can't do it. It's kind of fun doing something most people can't or won't do. The way we are, we don't scare.

"It's become a big business. It's changed a lot since my father and his brothers got into it in the 1920's. It's changed a lot since we got into it in the 1950's. New tracks have opened up all across the country and there are a lot more big races than there used to be and a lot less small ones. The purses have gone way up, but then the costs of cars have gone way up. The economy has cost us a lot of sponsorship support and it's hurt racing. But the driver is the same as he always was. He just gets in and goes."

Today he goes at around 225 miles per hour on the straightaway and, despite restrictions imposed on engines because of a series of serious accidents, circles the big track at averages close to 200 miles per hour. Lowering the levels of fuel that can be carried in a car has taken a lot of the racing out of racing and reduced many races to a battle of pit stops, but racing remains cruelly competitive.

The cars—low, wide, winged, gripping the pavement on wide tires, powered by supercharged engines—cost up to $100,000 apiece. Few will buy the "Foyt Ford" engines, figuring Foyt won't give them what he will give himself, so most run on $35,000 Offies, though there is a move toward cheaper stock engines.

"It costs close to a million dollars to operate a two-car team or a three-car team on the championship trail with spare parts and a complete crew," comments Parnelli Jones, the former 500 winner who put together the team that took Al Unser to the top, and who operated Ontario Motor Speedway when it first fell into financial problems. When Firestone withdrew from racing, Parnelli had to turn to Goodyear despite his long association with the other tire firm.

"Without Goodyear's backing, we'd be hard pressed to proceed," conceded Dan Gurney, the former runnerup at Indy, whose team took Bobby Unser to the heights.

Without free tires and parts, money invested in development, and the sponsorship support of the major automotive firms, the top teams would find it difficult to endure. New tracks have brought new races, purses have pyramided and winners can reap rich rewards, but not everyone wins. In 1970, Ontario Motor Speedway opened its $25 million plant. A year later, Pocono International Raceway opened its $20 million oval. Each has spectator sightlines far superior to those at Indianapolis. Each schedules 500-mile annuals for Indianapolis cars. Each pays out a purse of close to $400,000, with the winner netting around $100,000.

Still, Indianapolis reigns supreme. It never reveals exact attendance and receipts, but its race-day crowd of around 300,000 persons is three to four times that of the others and its present purses of more than a million dollars, with the winner netting around a quarter of a million, are more than twice that of the others, making it easily the greatest single-day annual sporting event in the world.

The success of stock-car racing has spawned a series of super speedways through the South and Southwest and produced high-paying, closely competitive spectaculars that are digging deep into the Indianapolis domination of this sport. Foyt, for one, has been drawn deeper and deeper into this tour. The dragsters seemed to have hit a peak of popularity. The Grand Prix tour remains glamorous; Andretti, for one, has been drawn to it.

Yet, Indianapolis endures, its tradition triumphant over rivals, its hold on participants and public alike a powerful one. Says Bobby Unser, "If you want to talk about prestige, Indianapolis is it. If you want to talk about money, there's a million dollars up for grabs there. No other place puts that sort of loot up. If you want to talk about attendance, there are three or four hundred thousand people at the race there. The crowd is bigger than the city I live in. You'd have to count all the cats and dogs and chickens in my hometown to amount to that."

Says Al Unser, "There never has been and never will be anything at all like Indianapolis. Not the Daytona 500. Not the Grand Prix of Monaco. Not any other race. Our family loves the Pikes Peak Hill Climb. There's nothing quite like it. It's unique. But it can't compare to Indianapolis. We're a racing family. We're happy to have the California 500 and the Pennsylvania 500. They've added a lot to our tour. But for a racer, the season is Indianapolis. Anything else is gravy."

His has been the most remarkable of racing families.

Father Jerry and Uncles Louis and Joe Unser were born in Illinois and reared in Colorado. They used to fool around with motorcycles for fun. They were there when the road up Pikes Peak was built and they built cars to race up it before races were run there.

Joe was the first to be tempted by Indianapolis and he was killed near Denver testing a car for the 500 in 1929. Louis never was tempted beyond the annual Pikes Peak competition in various classes of cars, and he won nine titles there. He was finally ruled off the road after forty-one years as too old at the age of seventy-two in 1968. He settled into resentful isolation in a house at the base of the great mountain. Louis seemed to resent it when his nephew, Bobby, surpassed him, winning twelve titles there, and then Al won two more. He did not speak to Jerry and his sons for years.

Jerry and his wife Mary had four sons—twins Jerry, Jr., and Louie, born in 1933; Bobby, born in February, 1934; and Al, born in May, 1939. "Pop" Unser, as he was called, ran garages, first in Colorado Springs, then in Albuquerque, alongside the highway through town. He built his home alongside the garage. Years later, the garage was torn down and Bobby built a home on that spot. Then Al built a home across the highway, on the outskirts of town, in hot, dry, lonely desert country, cars whizzing by their front doors. They moved in there with their wives, and started families there. But both suffered broken marriages. "The life of the race driver is very hard on wives and families. You're away a lot and always in danger," Al says. "It is hard for racers to hold marriages together."

Pop Unser set up cars for others to race and raced Pikes Peak many times without winning there, but encouraged his sons to race and supported their early racing efforts. They grew up fearless all-around athletes who fought freely with their fists among themselves, and together against others. Al and Bobby are competitive today.

"We're together a lot more at tracks than we are away from tracks these days," Al admits. "We argue a lot off the track and we're aggressive against each other on the track, yet we're close in important ways. In a race, he's just another driver to me and I'm just another driver to him. I'd rather beat him than anyone else, but if I can't win I'd like him to win. I'm sure he feels the same way. And if one of us is in an accident, it's hard for us to keep going until we get the signal that the other is all right."

Jerry became the first Unser to race at Indy. He and A. J. Foyt were rookies there in 1958. But Jerry crashed over the wall in a massive first-lap accident there that year, and was killed in a flaming crash in practice for the race the next year. Twin brother Louie won two titles at the Peak and raced on and off with some small success until 1964 when he was stricken with multiple sclerosis. He liked best to build racing engines, anyway, so he turned to that, and does that to this day at his own plant in Garden Grove, outside Los Angeles. Though restricted to a wheelchair, he is at the bigger races of his brothers. He sighs and says, "I've got determination like nobody has ever seen."

After Jerry was killed, a depressed Pop Unser retired from his garage to help and follow his youngest sons in racing. But he died of a stroke at the age of sixty-seven in 1967 before they scaled the heights. Mom Unser, however, goes to the top events to be with them, sometimes setting up housekeeping for them on the road, and annually preparing a red-hot chili feast for everyone trackside at Indy the week before the 500. A matronly, gray-haired lady, she has become a celebrity in her own right and often is asked for her autograph.

"I remember the first time I drove Pikes Peak," she says. "I was pregnant and daddy stuffed me into one of his cars and told me to drive to the top slowly. Why, I'd never had so much fun! I kept driving faster and faster," she recalls happily. "Whether it's Pikes Peak or anywhere else, racing is this family's life and no one ever knew a closer family. We've had our tragedies, but what family hasn't? I don't blame racing. I love racing, as our whole family has. I root for both my boys, but I root for all the boys."

Al says, "Mom has been an inspiration to us. And the memory of Pop. And the memory of Jerry. We were just kids when Jerry was killed. It hurt us, but it didn't hold us back. We knew he was doing what he wanted to do. We wanted to do it, too, and we knew he'd have wanted us to. Maybe if you're not made of the sort of stuff we are, you couldn't do it. We're different than other people."

Bobby says, "We were born to be racers. It runs in our blood. We have a gift for it. Actually, Al's more talented than I am. He's smarter and smoother on a racetrack. I have more desire than talent. I want it more than most of my rivals and that's what makes me better than most. I'm a charger. I can't stand to be second. Maybe I use up my cars that way sometimes, but that's my way. I've always gone as fast as I can as long as I can. I'm more mature now than I was and I practice a little more patience. Al's always had patience. He's always been willing to wait to take advantage of the mistakes of guys like me. I don't know which of us is better. I think I am. He thinks he is. Our styles are different. But both work. We're both winners."

Five years older than his brother Al, the taller and huskier of the handsome brothers, Bobby started first and got to the top first.

However, he traveled a long and uneven road to the top. He began in 1949 at the tender age of fifteen and had his share of reversals along the way. In 1951 at seventeen he was driving in the 2,000-mile Mexican Road Race with Pop as passenger and guide when he tangled with a car driven by millionaire Carlos Panini, who ran into a rock wall and was killed. Bobby admits, "I'll never forget it. It was not a good experience, but it taught me to be a hard person."

He got his first ride at Indy in 1963, but struggled with tempermental equipment there for five years. He crashed on the second lap of his first race and the first lap of his second race, but he refused to be beaten down. He was involved in the crash that claimed the lives of Eddie Sachs and Dave MacDonald in his second race, but Bobby says, "I refused to be psyched out. I refused to think about it." He drove one of the last of the Novis in 1965 and qualified it at a fast speed, but it failed him short of 200 miles. A year later, he kept running with a sick car until flagged off at the finish, almost 30 laps short of the leader. The year after that, he kept running with a weak car until flagged off 7 laps short. He had demonstrated determination, and his persistence paid off.

Finally, in 1968, he came up with a great ride in an excellent Eagle purchased from builder-driver Dan Gurney. That was the last year of Andy Granatelli's controversial turbine cars, which were faster than Bobby's piston-powered machine. Bobby became the first man through the 170-mile-per-hour barrier for a lap in qualifying at Indy that year, but Joe Leonard and Graham Hill in turbocars surpassed him before the day was done. In the race, however, Unser outdrove his rivals, passing superbly. He was well ahead of Hill when Hill crashed out. And he was running alongside Leonard until the gearbox in Bobby's car began to come apart a little and he had to drop back.

Al was driving Indy by then. Early in the race his car slipped out of control as the front end tore loose, he broadsided into a barrier, and his car came apart in pieces. The wheels ripped off and bounced around the track, and metal shot through the air. The other drivers, including Bobby, drove through the debris. Somehow, no one, not even Al, was seriously hurt. When Bobby got a signal from Al's pits that his brother was all right, he breathed a sigh of relief and resumed his chase.

Seemingly, he was hopelessly behind with only 20 miles to go when suddenly a ball-bearing broke in Leonard's gearbox and his turbocar coughed and died. Seeing Leonard coasting into the infield, a stunned Unser said, "C'mon Bobby, let's go while the sun is shining," and sped past to the victory.

His gearbox had given him trouble all afternoon, but it had not given out. He had a hard time accelerating back to speed after each pit stop, but he drove so well once he was at speed that he made up a lot of lost time. "I was lucky," he conceded in Victory Lane, his handsome face split with a wide smile. His good luck brought his team $177,000 out of the $712,000 jackpot. He won four other events on the title trail that year and his first national driving crown.

Al began driving at eighteen in 1957 and had many reversals along the way, but he progressed faster, soon caught up to Bobby and soon passed him. Baby brother, as he was regarded, broke in at Indy in 1965 driving for A. J. Foyt, went steadily and finished ninth. He wrecked in 1966 while running third with only 100 miles left. Then he finished second to Foyt in 1967, two laps back, but with an impressive performance. He crashed out of Bobby's winning race the next year and confesses, "I was happy for him, but jealous of him. You want your brother to do good, but I guess you're not human if you don't want to do better. We both wanted to be the first Unser to win Indy and he got there first." However, Al did win five times on the title trail that year.

In 1969, Parnelli Jones and his business partner, Vel Miletich, signed George Bignotti as chief mechanic and Al Unser as lead driver of their new team, and they came up with a hot car that was figured as the favorite for the 500 that year. However, Al broke his leg driving a motorcycle in the parking lot the day before qualifying began. He had been balancing on the back wheel of the bike when it toppled over on him, but he will deny to his death his guilt. "I wasn't fooling around. I wasn't trying to do a 'wheelie.' But I did one. I ran into a rut and the bike stood up on its rear wheel and went over." The gear-shaft lever arrowed his ankle.

A month later, he sawed off the cast and was driving again, and he won five more races on the championship trail, but he'd missed the big race, won by Mario Andretti, with Dan Gurney second and Bobby third. The masterful little Italian-born Mario had twice taken the pole position at record speeds, but was in his sixth attempt at the Speedway before he finally won one, and he has not been able to win another one since. Andretti won nine times on the title trail that year for his third national driving crown. He has won more than thirty times in his career in this competition, second only to the fabulous Foyt, but the sort of immortality that goes with winning Indianapolis more than once has so far escaped him.

Al says, "Missing Indianapolis that year was the biggest disappointment of my life. I'd not only let myself down, but everyone who'd worked on the car. It's not that often that you have a car that can win there, and if you don't give it a chance, you've wasted a wonderful opportunity. Fortunately, opportunity knocked for me more than once, but I'll never get back the one that got away in 1969." The car, driven by Bud Tingelstad, failed late in the running, but never ran with the leaders. Driven by Al, it might have been another story.

However, the following year, Bignotti and Parnelli produced a "P. J. Colt" car that was even better, by far the best car in the competition that year. From year to year, these masters of machinery improve their product. One always gets ahead of the others. Bignotti often is ahead of his rivals and he was well ahead that year, 1970. The car was sponsored by the Topper Toy Company and named the "Johnny Lightning Special," after the model racing outfit the firm was marketing.

Al led all rivals through the month of May and took the pole position at a speed above 170 miles per hour. Then, on race day, he dominated this classic carnival of speed, leading 190 of the 200 laps and winning by 32 seconds over Mark Donohue in a Roger Penske car. The total purse topped $1 million for the first time and the winner's share topped $250,000 for the first time. Al's team took home $271,000. The normal driver's share is 40 percent of winnings, but with bonuses Al earned about half.

"The money's super, but when you win, you don't think of the money you won, you think of being the best," Al said. Bobby thought he was the best, but he finished far back in this one.

Even in defeat other teams often come away from the classic with ideas that will make them the best. New Zealand's brilliant Bruce McLaren came away from the race with imaginative ideas for a better car, which would be aerodynamically superior to the rest. He wanted to move much of the weight amidships, use a wider, lower chassis and use a horizontal wing on the rear end to improve traction. He outlined his idea to Penske. Even as McLaren was killed test-driving a new car, others were carrying out his ideas.

At the inaugural California 500 in Ontario in September, Al was far ahead with only 35 miles left when his turbocharger failed. He coasted in despair into the infield, parked, got out, and walked into the pits where Parnelli and Bignotti waited. They shrugged and said nothing to one another. What was there to say?

Al changed into civvies and they packed up the car and were on their way to the next race before the results were announced. All the fast drivers failed that day, Bobby and A.J. and all the rest, as the heat and dust of the day extracted a severe toll, but a Foyt car won because a conservative chauffeur, Jim McElreath, ran just hard enough to outlast those that ran too hard.

Al kept running hard all year and he had a super year, tying

Foyt's single-season record with ten championship trail victories. Al set a new mark with almost half a million dollars in earnings in the one campaign and he added to it with considerable cash from commercial endorsements.

His manager, Chuck Barnes of Sports Headliners, Inc., observed, "The top race drivers can make more money than most athletes because their sport lends itself to endorsements. No one can capitalize on football and baseball and basketball the way the companies that sell fuel and tires and spark plugs and shock absorbers and so forth can on car racing. The top drivers like Andretti and Al and Bobby are worth a quarter-million in earnings annually before they even turn a wheel, and if they have a winning year they may make a million. The drivers are the men that make it in racing."

Al and Bobby had become big businessmen, well dressed off the track and at home in conferences with millionaires. However, Al observes, "We're still what we always were. We get into the other because it's worthwhile, but it's not where we belong. We belong in the grease, getting sweaty, using our muscles."

Bobby adds, "The distractions of these side situations can be disastrous. If they interfere with your racing you're running a real risk. You have to keep your concentration to keep winning and keep yourself in one piece on a racetrack. Life was more fun before we were famous," he admits.

Al's team returned to Indy with basically the same car in 1971 and was shocked by the speed of the McLaren cars, one purchased by Penske for Donohue, two others run by the McLaren team for Peter Revson and Denis Hulme. Donohue soared over 180 in practice, but was surpassed by Revson when it counted, 178 to 177, on the opening day of time trials.

Al settled for fifth at 174 and admits, "We knew they were faster, but we didn't know if they were more durable. It usually takes a year or two to sort out a new car, so we figured if we ran hard, maybe they'd break down in front of us." So Al ran hard, harder than Revson or Hulme, and when Donohue broke down in front of him, Johnny Lightning struck again, winning by 23 seconds over Revson.

Meanwhile, Dan Gurney, second twice and third once the previous three 500's, had given up his hopes of conquering this frustrating track as a driver and retired to devote his energies to winning with his cars as a builder and backer. This was a break for Bobby, who was given one of the Gurney Eagles.

He put it in the front row in qualifying, but put it into a wall late in the race itself. Just as Al had a crackup that worried Bobby when Bobby won, now Bobby had one that worried Al as Al won. Bobby escaped with only a "helluva headache," and he ran trackside to wave as Al went past. "It was a comfort," Al admitted later.

Al had one other rough moment when two cars tangled in front of him. "Cars were going every which way. I didn't know which way to go. I thought I'd had it," he admitted later. "If I'd have hit one, I'd have been history. I decided to get off the brake and on the accelerator to try to sneak through along an inside wall. I shot through and was home free," he smiled. "I didn't make a mistake all day."

The eighth man to win Indianapolis more than once, heir to the history of such as Tommy Milton, Lou Meyer, Wilbur Shaw, Mauri Rose, Bill Vukovich, Rodger Ward and A. J. Foyt, he followed Shaw, Rose and Vukovich as the fourth man ever to win the 500 two years running. He hoped to become one of the rare ones who won three. He couldn't help recalling his 1969 motorcycle mistake which cost him his chance to have won them in succession.

"Luck has to ride with you," he conceded, picking up his $238,000 portion of the million-dollar payoff.

At Pocono, Al tried his Indianapolis tactics again, but it was he who broke down, at 80 miles, with a cracked oil pump. Pole-winner Donohue persevered to a narrow triumph by less than two seconds over Al's teammate, Joe Leonard.

At Ontario, pole-winner Donohue ran out of fuel and out of the race. Al led late, but his equipment broke. Leonard went on to win another 500 triumph for Bignotti, and with it he won the national crown, although Al did win five times on the tour to set a four-year record of twenty-five title victories.

Envious, Bobby said of Al, "Hooray for the super-driver, except what he really has on us right now is a super-crew." But Bobby's bunch, guided by Gurney, were at work improving the Eagle to make it competitive with the McLaren and Bignotti creations.

At Indianapolis in 1972, Donohue's McLaren, prepared superbly by Penske's crew, was dominant, and Al, aiming at three in a row, had to settle for second, with teammate Leonard third. Actually, Jerry Grant, in a Gurney Eagle, finished second, but was penalized ten places for taking fuel from Bobby's pit after his own tanks ran dry. Bobby had a lot left, his Gurney Eagle having gone out within 80 miles after he had put it on the pole with a record 195-mile-per-hour run.

At Pocono, Al had awful luck. Donohue missed the race because of an injury suffered in a sports-car crash. Al led Leonard home by three seconds in a spectacular test of teammates, but he was penalized a lap for having made a pass under caution signals late in the race. Sagging in disappointment later, he sighed, "What can I say? You hate to lose a big one like this in this way."

After taking the pole position, Bobby's car had caved in early.

At Ontario, Al failed fast. Andretti failed fast. Leonard failed. Foyt failed fast. Grant turned in the first 200-mile-per-hour lap ever run in competition by an Indianapolis car, but his Gurney Eagle failed. Bobby surpassed him with a run above 201 miles per hour, but his engine blew up in the race. Roger McCluskey recorded the victory.

Al didn't win one race all year. Bobby won the four he finished. He sped his superfast Eagle onto the pole in ten races, but they broke in race after race. He drove hard, perhaps too hard. The Pocono triumph that was taken away from Al cost him his second national title and provided Leonard his second straight.

Donohue retired at season's end in 1973, but when Peter Revson was killed in a Grand Prix race in a Penske car in 1974, Donohue returned. He himself was killed in a Grand Prix event in 1975.

Bignotti left Parnelli's team to take over Granatelli's STP team in 1973, and Parnelli's team couldn't get a competitive car together. Gordon Johncock drove a Bignotti-prepared Eagle to triumph in a rain-shortened, 133-lap Indianapolis race. Al, Leonard and Andretti all failed fast. Foyt failed fast. Bobby's and Grant's Gurneys blew engines before the race was half over.

It was a horrible year at Indy. Jim Malloy had crashed to his death in practice the year before. Art Pollard crashed to death in practice in 1973, and Swede Savage crashed to death in the race. Salt Walther was seriously injured in a crash. The accidents of Savage and Walther were as horrifying as any ever observed at Indy. Spectators were burned.

Afraid of fire and scared by the speeds being attained by the streamlined machines, USAC officials imposed severe restrictions on the cars, designed to lighten their loads of fuel and slow them down.

Bravely, Bobby Unser insisted, "It's man's nature to keep going faster, and it's wrong in racing to try to keep us in place."

Al shrugged, "They do what they have to do. There's no such thing as safe racing, but if you don't have it as safe as is reasonable, you don't race."

Foyt prevailed at Pocono, smartly riding the new rules into Victory Lane as he made one more pit stop than Roger McCluskey, then went by Roger when McCluskey ran out of fuel near the finish. The cars of Al, Andretti and Leonard didn't last long. The Eagles of Bobby and Grant broke before the halfway point.

Dallenbach brought Bignotti another 500 victory at Ontario. Andretti finished five seconds back. But Bobby led until his Eagle got sick. And Al led a while until his car cracked in the late stages. Leonard's car already had cracked. And Foyt's Grant had crashed on the opening lap.

In November, in the last race along the championship trail in 1973, on the paved mile in Phoenix, Bobby's Eagle clipped a car driven by Gary Bettenhausen, went out of control and careened into a concrete retaining wall. The impact was so violent it tore the car in half, broke Bobby's shoulder harness, and sent him skidding along the track in the cockpit.

Amazingly, he got out of the wreckage unaided and limped away. On examination, it was discovered that he had a fractured left foot, crushed left hand, six broken ribs, and severe bruises all over his body. Al admitted, "I was afraid he was a goner." Al parked his car for the day. Bobby was in and out of the hospital for three months. But when the new season started, he was racing again.

The California 500 moved to March in 1974 to become the first big stop along the trail. Foyt had come up with the fastest car, but Bobby's was best. Foyt's fast car failed fast. Then Bobby and Al engaged in the most brilliant duel of brothers in the history of the title trail. They exchanged the lead fifteen times. Bobby came across at the finish just three seconds ahead of Al. It was Bobby's second 500 victory, but both of Al's were at Indy, where it meant more.

At Indy in 1974, Al's car gave out. Bobby's Eagle flew fast, but not fast enough. Johnny Rutherford rode a mighty McLaren to victory 22 seconds ahead of Bobby. Foyt's fast qualifier folded in the lead with 140 miles left. Rutherford picked up almost a quarter of a million dollars. Bobby bagged almost $100,000.

Al, while winning only $17,000, boosted his Indianapolis earnings past Foyt's total to an all-time high of almost $750,000 in just eight years. Bobby stood a distant third at less than $500,000.

Al conked out early at Pocono. Rutherford won there, too. Bobby finished fifth. But Bobby finished first four times on the title tour, including once in one of the big ones, the one at Ontario, and with these took his second national crown. At the advanced age of forty, he now had two of these tour titles to one for Al. And he had won nine times in the preceding three seasons, while Al had won only twice. At the moment, Bobby was hotter, and he insisted he still had time at the top. "I don't feel forty," he said. "I feel fine. My eyesight remains perfect. My reflexes are sharp. My desire is as high as ever. I may not pull over to the side until I'm pushed."

At thirty-five, Al felt much the same. "I've run into a little hard luck lately. My equipment hasn't been the best. But I still believe I'm the best. I'm not going to give up. This is what I want to do. The only thing is, I want to win." He had won more times by far than Bobby on the heartbreak highway they call the championship trail, 28 times to 21 times for Bobby. Al had moved ahead of Rodger Ward into third place in all-time total victories and was within reach of Andretti's array of 32 wins. Only Foyt was out of reach. And Al still could join Foyt as a three-time winner at Indy. He had two of these most coveted of crowns, anyway, while Bobby had only one.

Foyt's Coyotes still were running at superior speeds as the 1975 season started. He beat out Bobby in qualifying and in the race at Ontario. Al's car quit on him before he had gone 60 miles. He got out of the car, got his gear together, and got on a plane headed for home. However, he was headed for Indianapolis really, eventually. He always was. They all always are. It is the one place all racing drivers hope to make right all that has gone wrong with their lives and careers.

"It's a frustrating life, racing," Al admitted. "You may be the best man, but if you don't have the best car you won't win. The one you want to be best in more than any other, the one you want to win most is Indy. I'm one of the few who's won it more than once. I'd like to beat it again, but it's a hard place to beat and it's beaten me more than a few times, that's for sure. Bobby's beaten it, but it's beaten him more times than he's beaten it. A few of us have beaten it a few times, but it's beaten all of us a lot of times.

"The thing is, though," he said, "that is *the* 500. There are others, but that is *the* one. And when you're a champion of the 500, you are a champion all the rest of your life."

Al did not say it, but one thing he was saying was that if a man can beat that tough track more than once, if he can conquer that cruel oval two or three times, then he will be remembered as a champion forever. And when one whips it a fourth time, then he will have risen above the best of the brave drivers who have risked their lives at this shrine of speed.

At Indy in 1975, Al's car was not competitive, but Bobby's was. The year before, Gurney's Eagle had brought Bobby home behind Rutherford. Bobby's earlier victory here had been in an Eagle built by Gurney, but not prepared and put on the track by him. After thirteen luckless years as a driver and owner here, the popular Gurney, an influential figure in the history of this ancient arena, had yet to beat this hard race, and he hungered for it.

As 1974 had been, 1975 was supposed to be the year Foyt finally won his fourth at Indy. He had beaten Bobby out for the pole position and in the race to the checkered flag in California. Now, he unveiled a new car he considered even faster and beat Bobby out for the pole in Indiana. Gordon Johncock beat Bobby, too, in a new Wildcat built by Bignotti, moving Bobby in Gurney's Eagle to the outside of the front row.

Young Tom Sneva in a mighty McLaren was fourth fastest. Defending champion Rutherford in another McLaren had to qualify before some problems could be sorted out, but he still started among the front-runners. Wally Dallenbach in another Wildcat blew an engine in a qualifying attempt the first day and had to start far back after making the starting field on the second day of time trials, but his car, too, seemed swifter than Unser's.

But Bobby's car was the best.

While his proven car rested in the garage, Foyt gambled on his new car and lost. Although it took the pole, the new car never performed as smoothly as the old one had. Although Foyt took the lead in the early laps after Johncock's Wildcat fizzled out, Foyt's

infant Coyote was cut down by Dallenbach in the other Wildcat at
150 miles. Dallenbach was 20 seconds ahead and well on his way
to winning when fate intervened on the 127th of the scheduled 200
laps.

Passing another car, Sneva's car tapped it and was sent barrel-
rolling into an outer wall on the second corner, the car coming
apart in flames as it smashed off the barrier and went skidding to
a stop in a steaming pile of debris. Within seconds, Sneva had
been pried from the wreckage, suffering severe burns.

Coming on it, others were startled. Dallenbach drove down off
the track onto the grass, revving his engine so sharply he burned
out a piston. Rutherford and Unser snaked safely by.

"It was a terrible-looking thing, a hell of a bad wreck," Bobby
recalled later. "I had a snap decision to make and I dove low,
hoping Sneva wouldn't bounce all the way to the bottom of the
track. I got a little sideways and almost spun before I straightened
out and darted past."

As Dallenbach's engine expired, Rutherford rolled into the lead.
But Rutherford was due for a pit stop for fuel, and as he went in,
Unser went past on the track and into the front spot, the only man
to have been on the lead in all of the last five of these events.

When Bobby was breaking track records, capturing pole positions and leading races until his cars caved in, he was running so
hard his cars could not be kept together. When in 1974 he and
Gurney agreed to compete more conservatively they began to
come on. Others broke records and sat on the pole. Others led
early, but Bobby began to win late. His cars stayed in one piece
and he was close enough to win if the leaders' cars came apart.

He had, of course, finished first in California and second in Indiana in 1974. And he had finished second in California and now
he was about to finish first in Indiana in 1975. He had hung close
to the pace and waited for the right time to move. He had con-
served fuel and advanced to the lead in good shape for a torrid
stretch run that was never to come. No one will ever know if he

would have endured in the lead, because the fateful last miles were washed away.

Most of the day had been horribly hot and humid with the track blistering at 140 degrees and the drivers melting in their heavy, fire-retardant garb. Nearly 100 of the record crowd of more than 300,000 fans had been treated for heat exhaustion, but the drivers had persisted in their baths of perspiration. Now, suddenly, storm-clouds blew black over the oval.

About fifteen minutes after Dallenbach's engine died, the black clouds burst and released a deluge that flooded the course almost at once, causing the cars to become boats, skimming wildly over the water. Officials put on the yellow signals, but hesitated to turn on the red which would have halted the cars and sent the standings back to the preceding lap.

Unser slowed down sharply, but dared not slow so sharply Rutherford might risk a watery run, catch and come by him. As Steve Krisiloff's car spun around and around just short of the finish line, Bobby Unser again took the low road safely, coasting past on the inside of the flooded oval as the checkered and red flags flew above him. Behind him several cars slid and crashed. Then Rutherford came across. Later, Foyt got in.

Bobby's brilliant blue Eagle had led only 11 laps, but they were the last 11 of the 174 completed before the contest was curtailed at 437½ miles and the win was worth $214,000. It was the fourth time one of these Indy events had been stopped short of the full distance and the fourth victory for a driver forty years of age or older. It brought Gurney his first victory here in his fourteenth bid and it brought Bobby his second victory in his thirteenth try.

Ironically, later in the season, Bobby and Dan disagreed on how many races to run and how hard to run them. They broke up. Still looking for his first victory at Indy, Dallenbach joined Gurney. Joining another team, Bobby crashed in his first race in his new car and fractured his knee. But before the season ended, he was back behind the wheel of a racing car. Well, Indy had been happy for him this year.

Becoming the ninth driver in the history of this classic contest to win it more than once, the forty-one-year-old Bobby joined brother Al as a two-time victor at Indy. Depressed by his own defeat, Al summoned a smile to point out, "If Foyt couldn't win his fourth, at least the Unser family now has won its fourth."

Ignoring the downpour in Victory Lane, Gurney was gleeful. "I have never forgiven Bobby for beating me out in 1968, and I never will"—Dan smiled wistfully as the rain pounded down— "but I am grateful to him for helping me beat this place at least once at last." And he pressed through the throng to embrace the winner.

As the losers sadly walked in disappointment through the downpour back to their garages and began to gather their gear, a drenched winner pulled off his helmet mask, sat on his soaked racer, and said, "To beat this place once is something. To beat it twice is something else. We were good, but we also got the breaks."

Bobby Unser said, "Whatever else you have on a racetrack, if you don't have luck, you don't win. At this racetrack, in this long, fast, hard race, luck means more than it does anywhere else. You also have to be better than you are anywhere else. I think we were the best today. But we also were lucky today."

As always, luck had played a part, as well as persistence, skill, shrewdness and daring in overcoming the overwhelming odds against capturing this cruel race even once to say nothing of more than once.

Index